I.E.

An Autobiography

by

MICKEY ROONEY

I. E.

An Autobiography by Mickey Rooney

G. P. PUTNAM'S SONS, NEW YORK

For you, Mother

Contents

I.E.

An Autobiography

by

MICKEY ROONEY

1 * _All Right, I'll Talk_

I've got a bright idea for the start of this book.

Once upon a time . . .

The Hell with That.

This isn't a once-upon-a-time story, although it might have been. Lord knows but it might have been. Had I been brighter, had the dice been hotter, had the gods been kinder, this could have been a one-sentence story. Once upon a time Mickey Rooney lived happily ever after.

As you will see, this is a true story. It isn't _The Children's Hour,_ or _Portia Faces Life_ and, for that matter, it isn't _Hamlet,_ either. I'm sorry about that. I meant to write _Hamlet._ Somebody else beat me to it.

What is my story, then? You have a right to ask. A book ought to have some excuse for being written. Even if the book is a detective story, the reason should not be kept a mystery from the readers.

My story may answer your questions and correct some

misconceptions. If it hurts anyone, including myself, I'm sorry, but anyone who gets hurt, still including myself, probably deserves it.

My story is a tale of four disasters. Every unsuccessful marriage is a disaster, and I've been divorced four times. Divorce is not like the obstacle course in infantry training. It doesn't get easier because you've gone through it before.

My story is a love song to show business, sung at times off-key. Show business is my business, my hobby, my oldest mistress, my strongest crutch, my most enduring love. An audience's laughter and tears are as necessary, and as vital, to me as your own laughter, your own tears are to you.

It's the paradox of a child who was a man and a man who was, or tried to remain, a child. At the age of fifteen months I was working in burlesque and by the time I was two, I was ad-libbing scenes. But at thirty I was still shockingly immature, a con man's delight, a con woman's pot of gold. The honey pot of Hollywood.

Then, too, my story is probably like your own because we are both members of the race the skeptics condemn. My story, as yours, is a tantrum of anger, a hymn of hope, a fire of life, a sunrise of promise, a winter of discontent, a torture rack of growing up. In my own particular, complicated case, the rack may be most important. Now at forty-four, after four marriages vowed and broken, two or three careers created and destroyed, one or two fortunes gotten and spent, I finally know where I'm going and who's going with me. I even know who I am, which wasn't easy to discover. I was born Joseph Ninian Yule, Junior, renamed Mickey McGuire when I was six, re-renamed Mickey Rooney when I was twelve, and what did you say your name was, sir?

I have been, in warm and violent moments of my time, husband to Miss Ava Gardner of Wilson, North Carolina. A very beautiful variety of Gardner.

I have served, too, as husband to Miss Betty Jane Rase, a lovely girl who was at the time of our marriage Miss Alabama.

Next came Martha Vickers, an ash blonde whose softness was to be a complement to my purported forcefulness. It ended in boredom for two.

Then came Elaine Mahnken, a beautiful, fiery redhead. Some years later, when the decree was entered, my lovely Elaine was in possession of a $125,000 house in Studio City, a $35,000 house at Lake Arrowhead, a motorboat, 2 cars, 3 dogs, 2 horses, a chicken, 2 cats and a turtle, but was minus one Mickey.

Shortly thereafter, I married my present wife, the beautiful Barbara Thomason. With four children, a lovely wife, a beautiful home and my career on the upswing, at last I think I've reached the hill of happiness, ascending from the vale of fears and tears.

During other moments of my time, I have been Killer Mears in *The Last Mile*, the messenger boy in *The Human Comedy*, Puck in *A Midsummer Night's Dream*, and Andy Hardy and Andy Hardy and Andy Hardy and

Andy infinitum. During the Hardy run, I was the movies' biggest box office draw for three years. Louis B. Mayer said I was a good little fella and patted me on the head, realizing about 10 million per pat in movie profits. It wasn't until ten years later that Mayer threatened to throw me out of his office at MGM. It was the biggest office in the place. I doubt if Sandy Koufax could have thrown a baseball out of it.

I've owned an airplane which my friend Herb Jeffries crashed near a cemetery at Needles, California. All they had to do was jack up the propeller and attach a new fuselage, engine and wings. Then the plane would have been as good as new. I've owned a cabin cruiser, which sank on its own. It was a handsome cruiser, white and swift. It could do everything but float. I've owned horses that may have been excellent in the water. They must have been excellent somewhere. They weren't at the track. (If there were more equity in the world, I'd own 73 percent of Santa Anita, too. That's what my investments there have seemed like.)

I've written songs and poems, won table tennis championships, talked cars with Henry Ford, walked with Presidents and slogged through an Army career successful enough for me to get a Bronze Star. I'm mighty proud of it too.

I've lived in mansions where the bathroom fixtures were made of sterling silver, slept in frozen tank ruts, run a bookmaking business from a hospital bed and lost $55,000 in a single night at the tables in Vegas. I can mention my

Bronze Star without feeling boastful, because, you see, I also hold the Royal Order of the Idiot, First Class.

What am I like? Stand before the glass and consider yourself, inch by inch, wrinkle by wrinkle, imperfection by imperfection, scar by scar. The enterprise is doomed to failure. See, here the glass is flawed. Or is it the image that is flawed? Or is the flaw in the vision of the beholder?

We are all different things to different people, different things to ourselves at different times. It is the actor's trade to be as many different things as he can. Am I Andy Hardy? As Andy, I cried, and when the director called "Cut," could slip immediately into a Charleston with Judy Garland. I'd like to think somewhere back there, way back, there was a real Andy Hardy; one that you and I believed in. (I should have listened to the Judge.)

What am I like? A question all but impossible to answer perfectly, but one which I hope my story, in its full length, can answer well. It's funny. The full measure of a man is perhaps the most complicated study on this earth. And yet, when the man is a public figure, almost everyone who ever took a psychology course, or who can pronounce the name of Sigmund Freud, or holds a press card, or knows someone who does, thinks he can measure the man, analyze him, X-ray him. It's funny. But it hurts.

I am, as you know from the newspapers, "a sawed-off comic," and "a much-married entertainer," and "a man who can never find the bluebird of happiness." Phrases ladled from a kettle of clichés. I have been getting my name in the papers for more than thirty years. My face has been before the public for even longer. So to begin, I will not say what I am like. I'll tell you rather what I am *not* like. I'd rather first erase distorted sketches. I'm not going to write this whole book with an eraser, but there are a half-dozen portraits of mythical Mickey Rooneys around. Let's rub 'em out, as they say on television.

1. Mickey Rooney has a size psychosis, or so they think. Stretching to my full height at dawn, I stand 5 feet 3 inches tall. If this were a world in which all wishes came true, I might stand 6 feet 3 inches. There would also be no war, no famine, no babies crying in pain, and no heartaches.

But, as you accept the imperfections of the world, so I accept my height. It did not crush me when I realized I could never play professional basketball. My ambitions never drove me in that direction. It doesn't crush me when shaving every morning I see a face entirely distinct from the face of Cary Grant. We all want to be rich, handsome, and happy, and if we were, we would then want to be richer, more handsome and still happier. Most of us dream a little but most of us also accept life and go on living, without being crushed.

Now if the public decided that I was an inept entertainer, that would be something different. That might very well crush me. Not all things are equally important. Size, in itself, is not overwhelmingly important to me.

Then why did I always pick tall girls? I am not going to assert any specific preference for a certain type of girl. I adore all girls, and bless the ones who had to put up with me.

When I dated a girl who stood 5-foot-3 and wore heels,

she towered over me by four inches. "There goes that runt Rooney with another giant," says a voice loud with ignorance. Some girls I've liked have been 5-foot-3, and some have been taller and some have been shorter. Some have been redheaded, some have been blond, some brunette. Variety, you know.

I'm not likely to be a head taller than my date because I have refused, adamantly and absolutely, to limit my romance to midgets. So here is my real size psychosis: I've never dated a girl who was 2-foot-1. Thank you, doctor. Now can I get up?

2. Mickey Rooney is arrogant. (Subtitle: Little man— Big chip.)

When I was fifteen and famous, the simperings and giggles of teen-age girls use to add fuel to the flame of pride. I was brash at fifteen, if brash means the love of doing things. I was constant motion; I still am. I could sing a little, dance a little, was fairly good at impersonations, and worked hard. I had as friends the lovely Judy and luscious Lana and had played Shakespeare and talked with President Roosevelt. Everywhere I went I wanted to meet people and strangely they wanted to meet me, to have my autograph, to talk to me. Everyone seemed to be aware of me at fifteen. Everyone. That's a pretty strong potion to feed a growing kid. Of course I was arrogant then. What else could be expected? A fifteen-year-old sage? You can't put an old head on a young pair of shoulders.

Now, almost three decades later, that brashness has gone, along with some of my hair and all of my earnings.

Can any man have such fluctuations in his career and suffer the pangs of four broken marriages and remain arrogant? Can a once wealthy man suffer a period of hardship and inactivity and remain arrogant? I can't lie to my mirror, and this book is my mirror. We all know it is hard to wear success, and it's even harder to bear failure. My life has forced me to learn to do both. The arrogance is gone, but the image I created unfortunately remains.

One day a stranger approached and asked if I remembered him.

"To be honest, I'm afraid I don't. Where did we meet?"

"Why, I saw you in *Love Finds Andy Hardy*," the man said angrily. Then he stormed off.

Mister, wherever you are, that screen only works one way. I can't see out from it. Aside from that, wasn't the theater dark?

I wonder about that man. I wonder what he said to his wife. Maybe he said, "I saw Mickey Rooney today, and boy, is he an arrogant little punk. He didn't remember the night we caught his picture at the Orpheum. How's that for gall, Henrietta?"

Let me set it straight for Henrietta and her husband and for everyone else who cares. I am proud to be an entertainer. I am proud to act well (as I am embarrassed to act badly). But pride and arrogance are not the same. I try always to retain pride. Life knocked the arrogance out of me long ago.

3. Rooney is difficult to work with. (Subtitle: Small man—Big Drive.)

Before my first day on the set where *Breakfast at Tiffany's* was hatched, the producer introduced himself and said he wanted to talk to me alone.

"I know you like to joke while you're working," he said.

I said, "Not only while I'm working, but before and after." He said, "Well, whatever it is, on this set would you mind not joking at all."

"What?"

"It might upset Audrey Hepburn. Miss Hepburn has to give her work absolute concentration. Nothing must disturb her. I'm sure you understand."

I understand. There is a story told of the famous Russian director Stanislavski, the father or the grandfather of what is now called method acting. According to the story, Stanislavski was telling his pupils how to bring on tears. "You learn all about character," he said. "Where character was born, where character's parents were born. You learn what character thinks, how character eats, when character sleeps, what character dreams, the way character makes love. You think and you concentrate and you study character and you know character and then—you *are* character. So when it is time for character to cry, you cry."

"But, Professor," a student interrupted, "suppose I do all these things and still, when I'm out onstage, the tears won't come."

"In that case," Stanislavski said, "you pull a hair in your nose."

I understand. I think any actress worthy of the name ought to know how to pull a hair in her nose. I am intolerant of people who claim to need six hours of silence before doing their work. Acting is an art form but it is also a job. As I am intolerant of the somewhat prevalent pseudo-emotionalism, I am also intolerant of incompetence, whether it be producer, director, performer, stagehand or flunky. In the sense that I despise incompetence, I am difficult. In the sense that I despise pretense, I am difficult. When I encounter someone who is both incompetent *and* pretentious, I become exceedingly difficult. So does anyone whose credo is professionalism. But working with entirely professional fellow performers is one of my greatest delights. When I'm on a set with a Jackie Gleason, a Tony Quinn, a Judy Garland or a Buddy Hackett, there's fun and laughter—and our work gets done, possibly even under budget.

So you see, Mr. Producer, I understand. Why not you?

It is odd to find yourself defending the fact that you like to have fun while you work. It is not odd at all to defend yourself against a charge of irresponsibility.

I was damned as irresponsible not very long ago after an incident, or series of incidents, involving Gentleman Jack Paar, America's self-appointed godfather. If I were in court (again), pleading, I suppose I'd have to say guilty with an explanation. You deserve that explanation.

I first played the Paar show one year after my marriage to Barbara Thomason, the present Mrs. Rooney, who is blond, beautiful and, incidentally, 5 feet 2 inches tall. Before the show, Barbara and I went to the Tail of the Cock, a restaurant on La Cienega, the Wall Street of Los

Angeles' thriving restaurant business. Barbara ate a steak. I ate stuffed olives surrounded by chipped ice, vermouth and gin.

As I say, it was a wedding anniversary. I'm touched by and touchy about such things. I wanted to conduct a small celebration. I wasn't nervous. I didn't drink because I was tense. I don't get nervous before I work. Just the opposite, I get exuberant.

When we left the restaurant, I was decidedly exuberant. I wasn't out of my skull. I was high, happy, free from pain, but not smashed. If I had been smashed, Barbara would have stopped me from going on the show. Or a cop might have stopped me in my car. Or I might have stayed in the restaurant and gone to sleep. I knew where I was and what I was doing, but the martinis had taken their familiar effect. It's a great world, ain't it, fellers? I love everybody. I mean, look, I don't hate anybody. I feel good.

On the show, I began by saying to Gentleman Jack, "You'll have to forgive me if I'm overly cheerful. It's our wedding anniversary, so excuse me if I seem happy."

"Happy?" Paar said, sweetly. "You're loaded." Under the white lights, it was still a great world, but I didn't love everybody anymore. Now I loved almost everybody.

A few minutes later, Gentleman Jack tugged at his pantaloons and asked, "What kind of a girl was Ava Gardner?"

"She's more woman than you'll ever know," I said. The answer was tactless and truthful. I think the question called for that kind of answer. I didn't say to Jack

"What was your first wife like? How come you got a quickie divorce?" So I wasn't as tactless as I might have been, although I was beginning to feel a little hate.

My comment ruffled Gentleman Jack. He squirmed, as though his undershorts had pinched him, and after that the conversation became double-edged. Finally, he asked me how I liked his program.

"I don't watch it often," I said. A small lie. I watched it and didn't like it.

"Well, then, I guess you'd like to leave," Paar said.

"There's no doubt," I said.

Exit Rooney, wondering where his rosy mood had gone.

I wasn't pleased, but neither was I in a white rage that night. I didn't know that after I'd left, Gentleman Jack had told an audience of eight million, "Too bad. There *was* a great talent." I didn't find that out until the next morning.

At 7:30 the next morning, newspapermen, telephoning to my home in Encino, filled me in. Reporters from New York, wire service men from downtown Los Angeles, columnists from all over, were ringing, filling me in and probing for reaction. I had two reactions, both reasonable. First, I wondered why, with the world coming apart, this little matter constituted big news. Second, I was sore as hell at Paar for taking a swipe at me after I'd gone.

These were not the reactions I reported to the press. One doesn't. Complete honesty is not the best press-relations policy, sensationalism being a natural product of most American newspapers. If you are going to be burned at the stake, you don't have to bring along your own jug of kerosene.

"Yes," I told everyone who asked, "I was a little high. Just a little. No, I'm not angry at Jack. Thank you for calling. Thank you very much."

Later I saw the papers: ROONEY DRUNK ON PAAR SHOW . . . . ROONEY WALKS—OR STAGGERS—OFF PAAR SHOW. The headlines were loud, if not entirely inaccurate. The stories under them confirmed something else. Paar had made no effort whatever to protect me. I do not excuse appearing on television without benefit of Bromo, but had I been in Paar's place, I would have protected the other entertainer. Gentleman Jack, I realized belatedly, was not looking to protect anyone. His career had been lusterless. When he got the late-night program, he was determined to make a score, to be noticed, to get publicity—any way and at any price he could. I was invited, for a meaningless fee, to help him out, to be his guest. I tried to help him and turned out to be his target. So I did help him, but what a helluva way, the way a bull's-eye helps a well-aimed rifle shot.

That afternoon I called Paar to apologize. "Jack, I want you to know I'm sorry."

"Yeah," Paar said, raucous and unpleasant. His manner changes when they take the cameras off him.

"There's no excuse for my showing up high," I said, "but actually we're not that important. This thing is getting out of hand. Have you seen the papers?"

"What do you want from me?" Paar bawled. (Of course

he'd seen the papers. He'd probably planted the stories himself.)

"I'm telling you I'm sorry," I said, getting loud myself, "but why did you have to make that crack when I left the show? I'd always figured show business people were like a team. You know. Help each other. Protect the team."

"Who the hell do you think you are, telling me how to run my show?" roared Gentleman Jack.

"Don't yell at me. I called to apologize."

"I don't give a damn why the hell you called."

"Don't yell."

"What are you, some kind of tough guy?"

"Where are you right now, Jack?"

He told me and I took off, out of the San Fernando Valley and over the hills for Paar's hotel in Beverly Hills. Red Doff, who was then my manager, and Ray Pearson, who was then my friend, met me in the lobby.

"Don't go up," Doff said.

"Why not?"

"You'll only make it worse."

"I can't make it worse," I said.

I walked into Paar's suite and there he was, wearing a chi-chi zippered jacket, and juggling a cigar. There were six or seven men standing around.

"Hello, Mick," Gentleman Jack said. "You know everyone here. Shall we talk in front of the fellows?"

"I'm not here to talk," I said.

Paar made a little gesture and the men faded out, as stooges will. "Sit down, Mick," Paar said, quickly, when we were alone. "I don't know how this thing grew to be so big and, anyway, why are a couple of guys like you and me getting excited about it?"

He'd gotten his publicity. What the hell, I figured, why get physical with someone sweating all over his cigar? (And why get physical with six stooges outside?)

The next time I heard from Paar was six months later. He wanted me to play his show again. Might as well be decent about it, I thought. I said, "Sure. Any time I'm free."

In the second appearance, I opened by saying, "Jack, it's good to see you for the first time."

Paar turned to the camera and said, "Mickey was nice enough to *ask* to come back on the show." To *ask?*

Well, the hell with Gentleman Jack. I'm not the only one he's played for a fool. Maybe it takes one to know one. But if my adventures with Paar make you want to call someone irresponsible, I'd suggest that you look for a toupee-ed man sweating on a fat cigar. Stay loose if you challenge him, though. Some of the stooges are rugged.

4. Mickey Rooney is wild. (Subtitle: Small man—Big motion.) Someone commits adultery in Vincennes, Indiana, and people say, "That's shocking." Someone commits adultery in Beverly Hills, California, and people say, "That's Hollywood."

The truth is that adultery is shocking only when the electric blanket short-circuits. Adultery occurs in Hollywood, and in Vincennes and in Des Moines and in London and in Paris and in Moscow. I'd guess it occurs at approximately the same rate everywhere, too. Anyone who insists that he is shocked by the fact of adultery in Hollywood is naïve or priggish. However, a cup of coffee with a member of the opposite sex becomes a budding romance in the columns. Also, for some reason, possibly based on the misdeeds of a few, Hollywood seems to some to be the home of undisciplined sex. This is false.

He's a wild little nut, people have said of me, and I wonder what the hell they mean by wild. Do I share the temptations that afflict and delight humanity? Of course I do. Do I sometimes find that, in the words of Oscar Wilde, the only way to get rid of a temptation is to yield to it? Of course. Have I gotten drunk, blown money on horses, thrown fits of temper and whistled at ladies? Of course. I've been an alive male for forty-four years on this earth.

Most of these years have been spent in that complex of Southern California communities which are often lumped together as "Hollywood." Hollywood, cursed, blessed by the illusion of glamour.

This is the town where I grew up. It's where I first sneaked booze before I was legally old enough to drink. It's where I had someone buy mutuel tickets before I was legally old enough to bet. It's where I've done the things most boys do, or try, and most men do, or try—things that can generally be classified as part of the urge to live and learn.

I make no pretense at monasticism. The old oaths to poverty, chastity and obedience have never been my particular dish of tea. Or bag of oaths. But wild? Not by my reading of the word. I've never worked for mobsters. I wouldn't know the Mafia from the Klan. I've never run at anyone else's wife. I have trouble enough keeping up with my own. I've never committed a criminal action. My life in court has been civil, which is to say uncivil divorce and alimony suits. I'm intense and I live hard and if I sold insurance in Vincennes, I'd have been the intense, hard-living, insurance-selling Mickey Rooney. But I don't sell insurance and I don't live in Vincennes.

I'm a Hollywood actor.

That makes me wild.

5. Mickey Rooney is a great or gifted lover. (Subtitle: Little man—Sir Lochinvar.)

Due to the fact that in the course of my existence I have been married to five beautiful women, the myth has been created that I possess, or must possess, unusual talents in the normal pursuit of pulchritude. I'm a good actor. I'm average in all other respects, but I do have a drive and work hard for what I want. I wanted to marry those lovely ladies and drove for it. Perhaps the very drive that won them, drove four of them away. I don't know. If so, I'm sorry. At least I know we are still friends and they are still to me—lovely. Remember, too, that our profession attracts lovely girls, so that even an unlovely-looking guy like myself can get lucky.

But I am in love with love. I love people and I love animals. I love to give love and I love to receive it. It's sad but strange that people change; animals don't. A devoted pet remains true. I guess that is why I collect animals.

I know Elaine tells the story of my sitting on the curb

crying when we came home and found our pet kitten run over, and of paying $200 to fix the beak of our pet chicken. If this is silly, sloppy sentimentalism, I stand guilty. I try to inject this quality of love into my work and characterizations. I've felt your return in your applause. If some of you love only that side of me, it's sufficient—a little is better than nothing.

6. Mickey Rooney was warped by a successful childhood. (Subtitle: Little man—Big psycho.) As far as I understand amateur psychology, childhood can have only two effects on a man. Either his childhood is unsuccessful and embitters him or his childhood is successful and warps him. (After that, he then marries a girl who looks like his mother, which is significant, or marries a girl who doesn't look like his mother, which is significant.)

I was as famous as fame could make you. So, I am told, was Mozart. The trappings of fame that surround a famous child never fully explain the man which that child becomes. Or do I look like Mozart to you? (Or sound like Mozart?)

National fame, which I had, is a sophisticated concept. Five thousand dollars a week, which I earned, is an abstract sum. A child in Hollywood can't really understand that he is famous in places he's never seen. He can understand that there is enough money for all his wants, but he can't really conceive of the difference between $5 and $5,000 a week.

I suppose I had certain unusual powers. Early in life I

was supporting my entire family. I starred in pictures, and the action could not begin until I was ready. You know where a normal childhood exists? In the textbooks that describe it. Actually, there is no such thing.

It is all a question of degree. My childhood was very unusual. Yours was probably somewhat unusual. Our childhoods do not fully explain either of us.

Did the boys of the great depression era have normal childhoods? Still these fathers of today are the same kids, many of whom went hungry, that fought the battles of World War II and Korea. These same kids have finished their belated educations and today are the bulwark of our nation. Theirs was not a normal lot. They were not spoiled by the vicissitudes of life. Neither was Mickey Rooney. Any spoiling, he did himself.

This erasing, or redrawing of my image, is negative, but it is necessary negativity. You live your days as a supposed celebrity, and people you've never met form impressions. The first thing to do is break the shell and pour the egg to common view. Whether good egg or bad egg— you be the judge.

So let us bury the mythical Mickey Rooney. My ex-wives can act as pallbearers. A few agents can dig the grave. I'll conduct the services myself.

There is a time to be born and a time to die. A time for silence and a time for revelation. I have sold a lot of papers and gladdened the hearts of scandalmongers everywhere. I've also helped many people in many places;

not all good, not all bad. You may want to know me, so I'll open my mind and jump out.

Everyone has things that he meant to do and didn't. My life is crowded with things I didn't mean to do, and did.

I write this in a comfortable house, which I can't afford. Outside sit two compact cars, which I can't afford. The house is maintained by two servants, whom I can't afford. My four children are looked after by a governess, whom I can't afford. Sometimes I think that since I can't afford a comfortable house, I might as well move into a mansion. As long as you can't afford things, you might as well get the best you can't afford.

I used to think that way. It was just that kind of thinking once that made me what I am today. For I am a lot of things. In this instance, I mean a poor credit risk. I've been expelled from two golf clubs, which is bad enough. I've also been expelled from the Diners' Club, which is ridiculous.

You see, when between ex-wives, managers and agents, all my earnings were being taken, I concluded that no matter how many thousands I ended up earning, I'd never have any money. Since that was how it was, I reasoned, I might as well spend whatever I got my hands on, as soon as I did get my hands on it, or, if I could float a loan, sooner. I forgot about the Government; a very serious mistake. The Government didn't forget about me. My tax disasters make for a long story. Too long. Many sorry returns. I'll elaborate on them later. It is too soon to impose on you a tale of horror. But at the end, for the real

Mickey Rooney, never mind carving R. I. P. Just put I. R. S.—but this story has a happy ending because I closed strongly in the stretch.

Money is something I've learned to live without. Entertaining is quite a different matter. Currently I'd say I'm in the second or third stage of my comeback. Somewhere someone once uttered a slick line about a comeback. He said, "What do you mean comeback? I've never been away."

I could repeat that line myself, except that it wouldn't be merely slick. It would be dishonest. I have been so far away that the only way I could get into a motion picture was by buying a ticket at the box office. I've been so far away that I was barred from attending an Academy Award dinner. I've been so far away that I've talked to myself about quitting acting to open a gas station, or a malted milk shop, or a window cleaning service. M. ROONEY'S. *Short windows cleaned cheap. Tall windows subcontracted. Impersonations fifty cents extra.*

A writer can write, a painter can paint, a composer can compose by himself. But an actor cannot work individually. He needs a script, a stage, a performing crew, a group of technicians and, if he has a normal ego, encouragement. During many of my early years, I worked at acting for fifty-two weeks a year. People would ask me when I relaxed. What they didn't understand was that my work was my relaxation. I was relaxing all of the time.

I drive myself pretty hard. I can work on a set for twelve hours, come home and work for another few hours on a song or write a new story idea. Acting, dancing, doing bits, comes easily to me. Facing an audience is not an ordeal, but a delight. These things are both my hobby and my work.

What's hard, what's not relaxing, is the other. What's hard and frightening and inexpressibly difficult is real life. Living, not acting, is the fiercest thing. Let me work my trade seven days a week, all year long, and I'm a relaxed and happy man. Give me a six-month period of inactivity and I'm tense and miserable. I've never taken vacations. I've been sentenced to them.

Opening night nerves? I don't know what they are. I love the public. I hold no fear. Where I need courage now and always is in meeting the private moments of existence.

When my career eroded under me, based on wrong advice, poor representation and my own erratic conduct, I'd go month after month without working. I think one year in the early 1950's I was employed for only three weeks out of fifty-two. This hurt. First, I'd lost my job. Second, I'd lost my hobby. Minus both, there wasn't much left.

What do you do when you're an actor whom nobody wants to have act? You sit around and worry and think and sleep and drink and chase and wonder where everybody is. Hey, where did all the old friends go? What happened to all the lively parties? You sit in your house and days become weeks and weeks become months and then the phone rings. You spring to it, imagining that an agent will say, "I've got a great part for you, Mick." That's what you hope you'll hear. What you hear is, Mr.

Rooney, if you don't settle your account with us immediately, we're going to place the matter in the hands of our attorney."

"Yeah, yeah. I'm trying to raise it. Gimme a day or two, will ya?"

"I'm sorry, but we can only give you till five o'clock. And no check please. We demand cash."

"Yeah, yeah, yeah. Go to hell."

After that there is more thinking, worrying, sleeping, drinking and wondering. M. ROONEY's. *Short windows cleaned cheap.*

I don't begrudge the dark moments that have intruded into my life. There have been and are and will be so many bright moments to balance. I remember learning to play Shakespeare under Max Reinhardt, and having fun with The Great Garland, and playing long scenes with the irreplaceable Lewis Stone, and laughing through a bachelor party before I married Ava, and making a soldier cheerful the night before they cut off one of his legs, and having him thank me long afterward for the courage I had instilled in him. I remember later doing some decent things on television, and entertaining in Korea, and still later working in good movies again and, occasionally, in old days and new, picking a winner at Santa Anita.

There have been black moments, but this isn't a black book, any more than because there have been golden years, it is a Little Golden Book. It's multicolored, many-mooded. It changes as the rhythms of my life have changed. What I want most desperately for this book to be, from opening to finale, is honest. A book that isn't honest deserves only one fate. Not being read.

You see, through the good times and the bad, I've developed a fairly honest understanding of the human animal. Or of this human animal, anyway. If all the times had been good, I probably would never have achieved any understanding at all. I don't know if you have to die to understand death. I do know that you have to live to understand life. When things go bad you learn harder and live more. The cure of adversity is unpleasant but effective.

I've learned, because I've had to learn, acceptance of the human race, including the molecule of it that is myself. I know that men are as lascivious as women and that women are as lascivious as men, only more subtly so. I know that we are all possessed of strange drives which frighten us, drives which no novelist, playwright or psychologist has yet completely explained. The drives exist and stir our beings and move us to great acts of good and evil. Some try to ease the drives with narcotics. Some try to ease them with liquor. Some try to ease them by lying to themselves. Some, perhaps the happiest, try to ease them with sex. We can ease the drives, but, this side of senility, we cannot eliminate them. We could not if we wanted to and, personally, I wouldn't want to.

As I say, the drives are frightening. They send us down uncharted ways. But sometimes the answer to fright does not lie in seeking the roots of our fear. Sometimes the answer lies in courage to do our best to live a good life based on the tenets of decency and conventionality.

Recognizing our weaknesses, we should not overindulge them, nor despise them. We are of clay, but if we cannot help, then let us not hurt. That includes ourselves.

I don't know why I've been married five times. I do know this: I have been fearless in my fight for happiness, and my search for love, tenderness and devotion.

And this, besides. There is a trilogy all mankind seeks in common:

Some one—a person to love.

Some place—refuge from the pressures of the world.

Some thing—music, art, or, by any name, self-expression.

My life, as yours, is the story of such a quest.

I will now pack my soapbox and move along. I'm going, Officer. It is time for Joe Yule, Junior, to come waddling onto a forgotten stage in a theater that has long since been demolished.

Come on, Joe, and speak up loud and clear. These people have paid their way in to hear you.

2* *Pal o' My*

Cradle Days

I

Before the crap games and the tax debts and the *femmes fatales,* there was a little boy standing on a stage. He was wearing a tuxedo and pretending that he was a man. "Ladies and gentlemen," the tuxedoed boy-man began, "I'm going to sing. I'm going to dance. I want to spend my whole life entertaining you, and I'm going to start right now."

In darkened rows, the people sat expectant. They were not a chic, sophisticated audience. But they knew what they wanted and so, intuitively, did the little boy. Nose-high to a footlight, the boy began a sentimental song. Then, as the orchestra subsided, he broke into his golden-bantam recitation:

What would I give if I could erase
Each little wrinkle on your darling face?
Put there through sorrow, worry and care,

And sometimes I think it was I put them there.
Mother, oh, Mother, I'd give half my years,
If I could recall all the sighs and the tears,
The nights that you spent just worrying about me,
Wondering, wondering where I could be.
Then came a day when my heart filled with gloom,
As I sat, brokenhearted in my hotel room,
I needed someone to chase my despair,
But none of my fair-weather friends seemed to care.
Then came a letter, all blurred, like with tears,
With crosses and kisses saying I've missed them for years.
I'm coming, my dear, just as fast as I can
And won't you forget I'm a full grown-up man,
Caress me and fondle me. Fill me with joy.
For I want to be just your own baby boy.

When the child finished this recitation on that night
decades ago, there wasn't a dry eye in the house. Well, not
exactly. The child's eyes were dry. What the hell. I was
three years old. I'd been doing the cradle-days bit for
fifteen months.

That was how it was in the earliest days: songs, patter,
routines and, always, an audience. From as far back as I
can remember, there were audiences. From as far back as
I can remember, I was on.

My father, Joe Yule, Sr., was born in Edinburgh, Scot-
land, but grew up in Greenpoint, a section of Brooklyn
which was last green in 1685. More recently it has been as
green as asphalt. In Brooklynese, it is called Greenpernt.
It isn't far from Williamsboig. Rough, tough and poor.

I don't know how my father first fell into show business,
but I suppose he always had the flair. One day in 1917, his

mother gave him a dollar for groceries and a funny thing happened to Joe on the way to the grocer's. He enlisted in the Army of the United States. Two years later when he came back, he had a package under one arm. "Here, Ma," he said. "Here are your groceries."

My father was short, sandy-haired, glib, devoted to show business, fond of camaraderie, and life. He learned show business the same way I did—from the bottom, struggling to move higher.

My mother, Nell Carter, was born near Kansas City, Missouri, and before and after I arrived, she was what was then termed an "end pony" in burlesque. As burlesque was run forty years ago, twelve tall girls danced in the back row, and twelve short girls danced in the front row. The tall girls were show girls. The short girls were ponies. My mother worked end position, front row. Thus the name. End pony.

Mother abandoned Kansas City while she was still in her teens and hit the road with a show called *Bobby Barker's*. The troupe consisted of six girls, Bobby Barker, who was a comic, and Barker's brother, who played piano and, in a few skits, played a dope. I understand he could double, too, and play a dopey piano player. There was also a four-piece band. The band was not the Philharmonic and the company was not the Old Vic. Still, for a Midwestern girl who loved to dance and entertain, it was a start.

A start toward where? This was a long time ago. A start toward the Indian country, it turned out. In those days, years before the First World War, show business was entirely different from what we know now. Movies were an embryo or an infant. Radio had been invented—you could tap out SOS on a wireless, but that was about all. Television? There was no such monster. Almost all the entertainment was live, and in person.

Booking agents, working with performers and with theaters, had organized the country into circuits. The agents signed individual acts—comics, jugglers, acrobats, talking dogs—and put them into "teams." Live entertainment— entire shows—went by train to most of the big cities. The performers traveled to the audiences. Now, of course, live entertainment goes only from Beverly Hills to TV studios in Los Angeles. After that, electrical impulses do the traveling. Progress, I suppose, but something has been lost.

Bobby Barker's was not the sort of show that could compete on a major circuit. For one thing, it wasn't big enough. For another, it wasn't good enough. So Barker took his show beyond the circuits into the wilderness. The troupe traveled miles of dirt roads in Oklahoma, playing towns that had only begun to be towns. Once they were put up at the ranch house of a white-bearded man known as Major Billie, who was himself a showman under the name of Pawnee Bill. Another time, Barker's show played fifty miles from the nearest railroad station. The limits were the limits of civilization. My mother never played Bryce Canyon, but only for one reason. There wouldn't have been anyone on hand to watch.

Barker paid my mother $14 a week. She does not remember whether that included meal money.

Ultimately, Mother beat her way out of the underbrush and scrub cactus. She was hired as end pony in *Jack Reid's Record-Breakers,* a group that broke what records it could on the Columbia Circuit. With the Record-Breakers she kept traveling, only now she visited bigger cities and saw roads that were paved.

Jack Reid's Record-Breakers was a burlesque show, but different from the burlesque of today. "You had to be able to dance," Mother says, "not just go out and show your body." She had to rehearse some of the dance routines for four weeks.

Burlesque, when my mother, my father and later when I worked in it, was similar to what we now call a variety show. Some of the jokes were raw, but not offensive. There were pretty girls in both the front and back lines, but you could watch burlesque all night without once being offended by vulgarity. There were hawkers in the aisles who told you that for the price of one box of assorted bonbons, which was a dime, you might be lucky enough to get anything from a pearl to a diamond wristwatch. You had to be lucky, the hawkers said. But no one ever was.

Most of the show consisted of so-called blocked scenes. These are scenes in which the action and reaction are blocked out and set for all time. The famous Abbott and Costello routine, "Who's on First?" is an example.

"Who's on first?" Abbott would say.

"Who?" the late great Costello would ask.

"That's right. Who's on first."

The joke, of course, is that the first baseman's name is

Wilbur Who. Abbott and Costello played the scene, at some length, the same way every time they did it. Comics today still play it the same way. Comics probably have been playing it that way since 1839, the year in which baseball supposedly was invented.

I'm explaining the nature of burlesque because, as you'll see in a page or so after I get myself born, burlesque was the backdrop for my parents' romance and was both my playroom and dramatic school. Your mother was in burlesque? What didn't she wear? Such lines have no basis in the true history of show business or in the show biz lives of the Yules. I have nothing against strippers—I've dated some—but my mother wasn't one, if for no other reason that the art, or science, or craft, or zippers hadn't been invented.

My father skipped the Indian country. Instead he cracked show business in New York. As I understand it, he was discharged after World War I, brought home the groceries, gave his mother her change in francs, went to a theater and got a job as a property man. Oddly enough, he was property man for *Jack Reid's Record-Breakers*.

My parents met when there was a mix-up with the clothing trunks.

"I need a costume," my mother said.

"All I can find for you is an evening dress," my father said.

"I don't want an evening dress. I have to go onstage. I need a costume."

"All I can find," he said, "is an evening dress."

My mother stamped off, furious, throwing a daggerlike look at my father. Dad told me years afterwards what he had thought at the time, Wouldn't that be a fine woman to take home and say, "Mom, meet the wife"?

The process took several months. Behind the curtain, while the orchestra played the overture, the boys and girls in the *Record-Breakers* used to dance. My father, reconsidering his first impression, began asking my mother for a date. She refused for weeks but, apparently, out of the refusals a sort of friendship arose and one night Joe announced, "Nellie! You're never going to be out of my sight again."

"Why?"

"I'm going to marry you."

There was that moment of silence that says more than words.

My father had picked his spot well. The *Record-Breakers* were playing Niagara Falls. A few days later they were married in a courthouse in upstate New York. The wedding was delayed briefly at the last minute. The judge had to take time out to sentence a murderer.

Next case. . . .

Show business, like all business, has its social balance and the marriage of an end pony to a property man upset the balance in *Jack Reid's Record-Breakers*. Reid was genuinely angry at my mother for marrying someone whose social station was beneath hers.

"The idea, Nell," he began to grumble.

"Mind your own business," my mother snapped.

Reid then turned to my future father and began berating him. The more he did, the more my future mother berated Reid. There must have been a lot of shouting. At any rate, everyone ended up sore. Soon afterward my mother quit and went with another show that traveled far and wide.

The new show was run by a man named Pat White and my parents hadn't been with him long when one of White's top comedians died unexpectedly. My father was a good performer, something Pat White seemed to sense very quickly. White walked up to my father the property man and said, "How would you like to become a comic?"

"Wonderful," my father said, dropping three props. "Great. Marvelous."

"We'll give it a try, Joe. We'll see how you work out." White paused. "And by the way," he added, "pick up those props. You don't start as a comic until tomorrow."

Before very much longer my father was first-rate, a featured performer or, in the language of show biz, top banana.

I entered this world via a roominghouse at 57 Willoughby Avenue in Brooklyn, five minutes before noon on September 23, 1920. Willoughby Avenue was slightly south of my father's old section and it was Greenpoint slightly more refined, but both the street and the roominghouse were less than fashionable. Brownstones in decline.

My mother worked in the chorus line until August, six weeks before I was born. For the final days, she stayed in the roominghouse and wore a maternity dress of her own design. My father's brother, recently out of the Navy, gave my mother three large black neckerchiefs. She sewed them together and had her dress, or at least her skirt. As I say, Willoughby was not Park Avenue and the Yules were not listed in *Burke's Peerage*. There was more fun than money, which reminds me of more recent times when I had more money than fun.

Somehow my mother and father raised $150 which they paid to a lying-in hospital as a deposit for a room. Installment buying. For $150 we reserve your room. Then you have two long weeks to pay the balance. What happens if you can't pay the balance? Why Madam, we keep the baby. Sign here.

I might have spent months in that lying-in hospital, but one day my mother read a newspaper story about another hospital at which babies had been switched. "I'm not going to have my baby at *any* hospital," she announced. "I'm going to have my baby here where there can't be any mix-ups." After a big row with the hospital, my father got his $150 back. . . . Not long afterwards, I was born in a back room of the brownstone roominghouse, three flights up.

Prior to my birth my mother experienced cravings for watermelon and chop suey. While she was giving birth my father experienced cravings for alcohol. I weighed in at five pounds seven ounces and, after the excitement eased, someone noticed that my father weighed in at two fifths, one pint. They found my dad singing Scotch airs amid a heap of clothing at the bottom of a laundry chute. There was a lot of Scotch in the airs, they said.

When I was four weeks old, Mother went back to work and my cradle became a tray of a baggage trunk backstage. Now, my father's attitude toward a third Yule at the theater was not a jubilant one. There were, of course, bottles, diapers and bits of miscellany, in addition to me, cluttering his small dressing room. "You and that kid," my father would say to my mother, "are gonna drive me crazy yet." Some of the stagehands at the theater were just as explicit after having burned their hands on bottle warmers. Oh, yeah, I forgot. I started walking at 10 months, and as soon as I did, Mother outfitted me in a camel's hair coat, with belted back, a feathered cap, long pants and a cane. My mother insists that once, when we were walking down Broadway, a policeman told her, "Get that midget off the street. He's holding up traffic."

I started talking when I was about a year old (I haven't stopped since) and my diction apparently was good from the beginning. For—once I could walk and talk—I was ready to hit show business. At the age of one? Why not?

Backstage was an unusual nursery, backstage with its bright costumes, its odd pieces of scenery, its funnymen, its lovely girls and, most of all, its unending sense of excitement. The moods backstage—instant triumph, instant failure—match the mercurial moods of a child. Applause, which is affection from strangers, is vital. An actor needs it, as a child needs applause and affection from his parents. Such parallels make backstage a good, if unorthodox, nursery. At any rate, I never played with blocks. I played with props and pieces of tinsel.

I wandered freely behind the scenes. There was no

danger of my getting lost, I could find my way around. I knew everyone in Pat White's show and, like it or not, everybody in Pat White's show knew me.

One day, when I was about a year and a half, I quit backstage for a new playpen. Clutching a penny whistle, I followed the orchestra to the pit, crawled into the pit, crawled onto a drum and began to go through the motions of playing. Burlesque was informal entertainment. The orchestra leader went along with me immediately. So did the audience. It must have looked pretty funny: an infant, dressed like a dandy, going through all the motions of being a musician. One comic later complained to my mother, "Nobody paid any attention to me, with that damn kid of yours hamming it up on the damn drum."

TODDLER SHOW STOPPER, *Variety* might headline. Pat White was so pleased he invested $50 for a tuxedo custom-made to my size. Forty inches of it—all of it. Mother still has the tuxedo; it would be too small for an adolescent chimpanzee.

For a while I was content to sit in the tuxedo on the drum. But I dreamed big and one night, as an actor was about to start "Pal o' My Cradle Days," I interrupted his routine. "Parden me, sir," I shouted, "I bet I can sing that song too."

The actor was doomed. If he slugged me, as he must have wanted to, he would be damned as a child-beater. If he didn't slug, or choke me, I was going to sing. I knew all the words to "Cradle Days." I'd heard them night after night.

"All right," said the performer, trying to smile. "Go

ahead and sing it." "O.K., I'll bet ya, sir," I said. "You have a wager!"

The orchestra leader handed me a five-dollar bill. I sang and, predictably, the audience responded warmly. Then I tore the $5 bill in two and gave half to the conductor. "We win," I told him. The results of this triumph—more laughter and cheers from the audience—moved me up from the drum to the stage.

Now they wouldn't let me start with a solo act, so a comedian named Sid Gold worked with—or above—me. Mr. Gold was a combination straight man and guide. Our routines, as I remember them, were chestnuts. None of the jokes deserves to be written on a stone. There was some patter, with Sid feeding me straight lines. After a few minutes I'd break into "Pal o' My Cradle Days." I always left 'em crying when I said good-bye. Or meant to. The truth is, the jokes alone would have left some audiences in tears.

On a day when we were playing a Ladies' Matinee (they were always *so* popular) I decided it was time to do some ad-libbing. Now let me tell you about the Ladies' Matinee in the old days of burlesque. A man with the price of a ticket wasn't barred at the door. In a Ladies' Matinee audience, you could always spot a few stray males, escorting wives, perhaps, or ducking the boss or, for all I knew, hiding from the police. But the audience was predominantly female.

Maybe the ladies felt a little naughty going to see burlesque, but there was nothing naughty about the show they saw. Ladies' Matinee was caution time. The risqué stuff, such as it was, got toned down. Everybody was on good behavior. I mean it was supposed to be a circumspect thing, if not exactly as blue-nosed as something you'd do before the annual convention of the Women's Christian Temperance Union.

Well, before this Ladies' Matinee audience, I strutted on to the stage, replete in my tux, and Sid Gold began his usual opener. "Sonny," he said, "why does a fireman wear red suspenders?"

The joke is as old as the hills. Probably everyone knows that the answer is "to keep his pants up."

But I'd heard a new word a day or so before, and it was going to be a part of my first venture into the extemporaneous. I looked Sid straight in the eye. "Certainly I know why a fireman wears red suspenders," I said. "To keep his jockstrap up!" Then I grinned.

The silence was deafening. I mean there wasn't just an absence of noise. There was a positive kind of silence, as oppressive as the inside of a tomb. Ladies' Matinee. . . . Jockstrap . . . ?

Still grinning, I looked at Sid. His jaw was slack. His mouth gaped like the entrance to the Holland Tunnel.

My grin was getting a little frozen now. A little forced. I looked offstage. My father was raging. I looked to the other side. My mother seemed just as mad. There were two choices. Get off the stage and face the fury, or stay out there and face the shocked audience. Like the poilus at Verdun, I stood my ground. After what seemed like eons of time, Sid Gold closed his mouth. When he opened it again, he whispered through a hoarse throat. "Sonny, why did the man put the puppy in the icebox?"

Sid's brow was covered with sweat. I knew I was in trouble. "Because," I said, "it was a hot dog."

After that incident I didn't ad-lib again for a long time.

As an infant actor, I traveled the circuit with my parents, playing the East and the Midwest and sometimes looping up to Canada. Home was always a roominghouse and roominghouses that boarded show people always had a rule. No cooking in the room, was that rule. Some silly worry about fire prompted it.

Often when there wasn't much money (which was often) my mother cooked in the room anyway. She traveled with Sterno and hoped. There were days when she got away with cooking in the room, and there were days when she didn't. Then there'd be a pounding at the door, some bellowing from the mistress of the roominghouse, and the Yules would soon be banished to the street. After a while my mother got used to the routine. Whenever she was kicked out of a roominghouse, she left carrying half-cooked food. Better to eat on a stoop-front than go hungry.

I had my own traveling bag. It was about the size of a doctor's kit, and I used to pack it myself. Through observation, you see, I'd learned about porters and I wanted to go first class. As soon as we'd get to a railroad station, I'd start demanding a porter, and frequently, a porter obliged. It must have made a curious scene. My father struggling with all our heavy suitcases. My mother carrying a bulky bundle of toys. And I, walking ahead like a prince, while a porter carried *my* valise, net weight 2.6 lb.

I don't suppose it was so funny to my father. After carrying all the heavy luggage, he still would be stuck for the tip.

Laundry, like meals, was a problem, but one more easily solved. My mother did the washing in the room. Then, improvising, she'd rig some sort of line, hang the clothing and open the window. I don't know how many mornings I awakened to see my father's long white underwear billowing in the breeze, like a malformed flag of surrender.

When eating on trains, I used to order as though the dining car was heading straight toward a famine. I'd heard menus and I'd memorized some pretty fancy dishes. I could say filet mignon at an early age. This too was funny to everyone but my parents, who had to eat cheese sandwiches while I feasted. The budget usually couldn't possibly stand three hearty meals.

The weeks before Christmas and New Year's are slow weeks on the road and, by tradition, everyone in the theater works for half pay. Merry Christmas. *And* a Happy New Year.

I don't know what psychologists would say about an infancy such as mine. Bad for the child, perhaps. Too much attention. Too little stability. Nonetheless, I know this. I had a hell of a lot more fun than if I'd been the son of a psychologist.

Sometime during these beginning years, my parents began to have their troubles. My mother found life as one of Pat White's Gaiety Girls an increasing strain, and my father found life, as head of a transient household, an increasing drudge. When I was about four, my father went to work in a stock company in Chicago and my mother went back to live with relatives in Kansas City. There was a good deal of commuting back and forth, and about four or five distinct separations and reconciliations. Later, I was to become an expert on separation and a student of reconciliation. At four, I was neither.

One day at the train station in Chicago, my mother opened the crocheted boodle bag in which she carried the family fortune. Slowly and carefully, she counted out the contents. Ten, twenty, thirty, forty dollars.

"Joe," my mother said, "we can't go on."

"What?"

"We can't go on, Joe. Here's half the boodle bag. Twenty dollars. Good luck."

Between them passed a long and poignant look. Between them, too, was another silence, a silence which, years later, would recur in my own life.

My mother and I went back to Kansas City and it was a long time before I saw my father again.

My mother was an enterprising woman. Although she was now out of show business, she still had to work. Chickens were cheap in the Kansas City area. Thinking fast, my mother decided to open a restaurant featuring home-cooked chicken and hot biscuits. She took in a partner, a friend named Myrtle Sutherland, and the two did a fair business. The price for a plate of chicken, biscuits and a glass of brew was twenty-five cents. It sounds to me as though the business was fairer to the customers than to the ladies who ran it.

Kansas City was where I had my brief and only exposure to a childhood that can be called normal. We lived in a house with a yard and a kitchen and an outside clothesline. The Sterno was packed away. My costumes were hung in a closet. I was just another typical four-year-old—except that I'd had two and a half years of acting experience.

It was all so long ago, but impressions of the Kansas City days are still with me and I can still remember so many things. Like this:

The incense of the stove burning hot on cold frigid mornings in Kansas City. The Cream of Wheat. The taste of cold water from the kitchen tap. The tin cup that would hold the elixir. The soft grass at 2221 Denver, that helped me stand the cracked cement that on hot summer days would burn my feet on the way to the store. Oh, yes, the store. There was sawdust on the floor, the aroma of freshly ground coffee, bananas, penny candy—wine balls, they were called. Fresh bacon sliced in individual widths by hand to the buyers. Gingersnaps and Fig Newtons. At home, warm summer evenings with the front door open wide. The sound of the tamale men calling out "Hot tamales, two for a nickel, four for a dime." The kerosene lamp with which you saw what he sold you. The smell of rain in the air—the sound of thunder in the distance. The whistle of a far-off train. The soap that washed my mouth out after the naughty word. The search for worms to go cat fishing with my beloved Uncle Wade, a big Lincoln-esque man. The musty smell of the riverbank and the bobbing red cork at the end of the pole. The many-colored lights that changed with the fountain sprays at Prospect Park. The smell of the inside of the streetcar. The gentle hum of the generator when the car stopped. The picture show. The popcorn. The deep sleep and gliding motion, being carried back home in my Uncle Wade's arms, late at night. My dog Siggy, sleeping by the stove or greeting us at the door when we returned. The echo of the depot as the trainmaster called out in a mono-tone arrivals and departures.

These are some of the things that still come back to me from long ago.

Instead of props, in Kansas City, I had to play with less colorful toys, and one day I was walking about with a wooden board from which nails protruded.

"Stop playing with the board, Sonny," my mother said.

"No."

The conversation continued for a moment or two. Then Mother rapped me across the hands. "Smarty."

A few days later a minister was visiting and Mother, discussing discipline problems, mentioned the incident. "So I struck him very hard on the hands," she said. The minister looked at me. "Did your mother have to hit you?"

"Yes, sir," I said, "but I didn't drop the board."

"More tea, please," the minister said.

So I guess I was stubborn. I suppose, too, I missed both the theater and my father. I had spent most of my four years learning how to entertain. Now where in the world had all the audiences gone? I talked about show business and my mother talked about show business and although she was a restaurant owner now, she still read *Variety*, the show business paper. Once she saw an item that Hal Roach, the famous producer, was looking for child actors.

"Myrtle," she said, "what do you say we go to California?"

"Where?" asked Myrtle Sutherland.

"California. I have a feeling about Sonny and the movies."

"When do we leave?" Myrtle said.

"Tomorrow morning."

Mother closed the business, bought a lean-to tent at Montgomery Ward, picked up an ancient car somewhere else, and sure enough the next day we headed west. We drove down back roads, through silver-mining districts, maybe covering the same wilderness my mother had covered years before with Bobby Barker's troupe. Since there wasn't much money, we slept under the lean-to every night. Along the way my mother bought food and cooked it out-of-doors. This was only a slight variation on cooking inside a roominghouse, and she handled open-air cooking without difficulty.

When something came loose in the engine, Mother had

to heat a slab of bacon and used the bacon fat as glue. The glue held perfectly until the engine warmed up. Three weeks, two days and six pounds of bacon later, we arrived in Hollywood. Did Hal Roach meet us? No! Did reporters interview us? No! As a matter of fact, nobody seemed to care that we had come at all. We had twenty-five dollars so it was embarrassingly clear that my movie career had better begin immediately. Or before many more meals came due.

Our funds were dwindling fast. I'm not sure just how my mother managed. Certainly she worked wonders with very little. But for a time it seemed as though she was caught in a losing battle. By Christmas, our first California Christmas, we were all but penniless. There wasn't even enough money to buy a Christmas tree. Mother, God love her, searched the neighborhood for a suitable branch, and somehow she found one, broke it off and set it up in our little living room.

Now we had a tree. For toys, Mother had been setting aside a special fund which I think totaled all of fifty cents. Now she went to a dime store and spent the half dollar buying what she could for me. Then it was Christmas. We were broke, lonely, without prospects, but it was Christmas. And we had a tree. And I had some dime-store toys. To me, at least, that first California Christmas, long ago, will always be the meaning of Christmas. It could have been gaudier, but it wouldn't have been as profoundly meaningful if the tree had been huge and all my toys were solid gold.

Solid gold? That was the feeling between Mother and me. I mean for a little boy at Christmas, one branch disguised as a tree, plus four cheap toys and a loving mother, equals happiness. Happiness on fifty cents.

I had an interview some days after that first bright Christmas. By now the children and their mothers were thinning out at the studio. Some had seen enough of show biz very fast. Anyway, one of Roach's assistants talked to me, then told my mother, "We'll try him out at five dollars a day."

My mother said, "Five dollars a day for my Sonny? He's worth two or three times that, and we haven't been out here all these weeks just to get an offer like that, why, I can always go back to the chorus line."

And she did, in Oakland. Joan Blondell and Glenda Farrell were in that chorus line with her. She was paid twenty-five dollars a week, or something less than five dollars a day. We'd played for big steaks and lost. Mother, please pass me the hash.

The Oakland job didn't last. Sammy Michaels, who ran the burlesque house, told my mother that he was under pressure to hire local girls. Mother had come from Kansas City. She was living in San Francisco, and commuting to Oakland by ferry. Two points against her. We went back to Kansas City as broke as we had been when we started. Nothing had been lost but Myrtle Sutherland, who dropped off somewhere along the way. But within the year we were en route to Hollywood again, this time to stay.

II

Myrtle Sutherland was on her own, but my mother had other friends. One of them, George Christman, who managed a theater at Twelfth and Walnut in Kansas City, decided to invade Hollywood, with company. He organized an expeditionary force consisting of two cars and eleven people. Everybody chipped in. My mother managed to raise enough to buy four tires.

This time we went west without a lean-to. Each night, the adults spread blankets on the ground and we slept exposed to rain and dew. However, Christman was a good navigator. We took a direct route and hit Hollywood in just ten days.

In the mid-1920's, newspaper comic strips, a fairly new medium, were becoming more and more popular. One of the best—it was actually comic and free of sex and violence—was something called *The Toonerville Trolley*. An artist named Fontaine Fox had created it.

(I feel my age. Children, trolleys were vehicles that ran on tracks and were powered by electricity from overhead lines. If you really want to see one, go to New Delhi, India, or Johannesburg, South Africa, where, I understand, some vintage American trolley cars are still in use.)

Anyway, the characters in Fox's strip lived along the Toonerville Trolley line. One of the roughest and most popular of what Fox labeled the Toonerville Folk was a tough little black-haired boy called Mickey (Himself) McGuire. There were no gang wars in those days, nor zip guns, nor young men clubbing one another with short lengths of cast-iron pipe. Mickey (Himself) McGuire wasn't a gang leader. But he was rugged. He was the toughest kid on the whole line of the Toonerville Trolley, which, incidentally, advertised that it met all trains.

This was a great era for child actors in short subjects and a producer named Larry Darmour decided to make a series of films about Mickey (Himself) McGuire. My mother had moved us into a house on Burns Street in Los Angeles, and was working as a telephone operator while waiting for my break. When she heard about the proposed McGuire series, she disconnected some people and hurried home.

She coached me briefly. She also found some black shoe polish and rubbed it in, over and through my sandy hair. Then we were off to the studio, which was opposite a cemetery. I took a screen test and three long days passed without anything happening. Then Mother called the studio and said, "I've got five other jobs that have been offered." It wasn't much of an exaggeration. Just five jobs' worth. (Where did she get her confidence?)

"Have him back at the studio tomorrow morning," someone told her. "We want to make some more tests." (It sounded as if I was at the Mayo clinic.)

Out came the dark shoe polish again, and Sandy Sonny was transformed into Black-haired Mickey. At the studio they had a costume waiting. Mickey McGuire, in the comic strip, wore an old derby, a checkered shirt and packed a stogie in his mouth. They draped me in a checkered shirt, slapped a derby on my head and stuck a stogie into my mouth. Remember, I was five, or at most six.

"Nothing to worry about," Darmour said. "It's a special kind, a fake—it's made of rubber." Thank heaven he didn't light the darn thing.

I moved under the hot lights and acted tough and talked tough, and fighting off the unpleasant taste of soggy rubber, I guess I passed.

My first two years were spent learning to love the people in show business. I'm probably one of the few people in the world who, in his maturity, can remember much about his first two years of school. I ought to. They were exciting, stimulating and unique. I learned to love show business people, and as I worked I was taught to love audiences. The teacher, of course, was applause.

So, I learned about love in those early years. Is there anything more important? And I acquired a kind of confidence, as well. This was the beginning of the confidence that helped save me from Lord knows what black and long years afterwards. I've had bad times, but while agents neglected my career, while wives became receivers of alimony, while friends became strangers, one confidence stayed strong inside. Never, in my worst days, did I ever doubt that I could go out and face an audience or a camera. That was a pretty important thing. Sometimes, in fact, it was the only thing I had.

The first few years were good years, in the balance.

They may have been a little hectic, but I always like to leave the matter like this:

—Mr. Rooney, when did you start working?

—When I was a year and a half old.

—And before that, Mr. Rooney?

—Oh, I just sat around the house and loafed.

3 * *What's My Name?*

I

These Hollywood operators knew they had a good thing and, like all operators in Hollywood, French Lick and Oconomowoc, their idea was to make the good thing better. Onward and upward, onward and downward. Does this bus go to Fort Knox?

Anyway, the operators were talking and I imagine the conversation went like this:

"These Mickey McGuire shorts are sockeroo, Manny."

"Yeah, but we got to find a way to make 'em super-sockeroo. You reading me okay, Alistair?"

"Yeah, Manny. Yeah. Yeah. Yeah."

"That kid who plays McGuire, what's his name? Easter? Christmas?"

"Yule, Manny. The little kid's name is Yule."

"Well, what the hell we paying the kid, Alistair?"

"Around a hundred a week."

"A yard a week, and he ain't ten yet. Maybe we should cut him to fifty."

"It'd be rugged, Manny. He's the star, and besides, we only pay him when he's working. It's not like he's getting rich from being McGuire. Maybe he pulls down four big ones a year."

"I'm telling you, Alistair, we got to find a way to cut expenses. Leave more in the pot for us."

"How about using cheaper film, Manny?"

"Look, Al, you're not thinking big."

There is a long pause. Alistair and Manny concentrate on thinking big. Suddenly, Manny jumps up, snaps his fingers and cries, in the original Greek, "Eureka!"

"Somebody goose you, Manny?"

"No, dopey. Don't you know Greek? Eureka is Greek for 'I've got it.'"

"What have you got, Manny?"

"An idea that will save us a thousand bucks a picture."

"Eureka, Manny."

"The guy who started *Toonerville Trolley*. What's his name? Lion? Wolf?"

"You're weak on names, Manny. The guy's name is Fox, Fontaine Fox, Manny."

"And he gets a grand every time we make a McGuire picture, Alistair. Ain't that right?"

"That's right. He invented Mickey McGuire so he gets a thousand-dollar royalty."

"Who invented McGuire, Al? Think, Al. Who? We invented Mickey McGuire, baby. You and me, we're the guys that did it."

"I don't getcha, Manny. We take the character from the comic strip and . . ."

"And we make him, Al. We make him a hero. He's our baby, Al. Now what the hell we paying a grand royalty for?"

"But, Manny, our character is based on the comic strip."

"Alistair, I told you once I told you ninety times. Think Big. We take this little kid Christmas. We change his name to Mickey McGuire. Legally. That way the pictures are based on this real little kid. We don't have to pay Wolf any more money."

"The kid's name is Yule and the guy's name is Fox, Manny."

"Don't confuse me with names, Al. Use your head. We make the little kid change his name in court and there's no more royalty to pay."

"Gee, Manny, that way the only name you'll have to remember is Mickey (Himself) McGuire."

"And Grover (Himself) Cleveland, Al. Don't forget Grover Cleveland."

"Why shouldn't I forget Grover Cleveland, Manny?"

"His picture is on a thousand-dollar bill."

Pin me wriggling to a wall and I'll concede that this precise conversation may never have occurred. But something very much like it did somewhere in Hollywood during the 1920's. While I was still in short pants, they changed my name from Joe Yule, Junior, to Mickey Mc-Guire, in order to beat Fontaine Fox out of his royalties.

The name change didn't stick, but I'm getting ahead of myself. Where was I, Manny? Al?

The McGuire series was a success from the start, just as later the Andy Hardy series succeeded from its beginning, which, by the way, was a 1937 quickie called *A Family Affair*. I think I made fifteen or sixteen Andy Hardy pictures. I have no idea how many Mickey McGuire shorts there were. My mother says seventy-eight. That sounds a little high, Mother. Fifty doesn't.

The movie Mickey McGuire was much like the comic-strip McGuire. Brash, wise beyond his years, and stubborn. So he was also much like Joe Yule, Junior. The early McGuire movies were silent and I don't remember the plots. I do remember the plot of *A Midsummer Night's Dream*, in which I played almost as long ago. If they'd written the McGuire movies the way Shakespeare wrote *Midsummer Night*, I'd remember them, too.

With the first McGuire pictures, I began to make a living for my mother and myself. I didn't earn a great deal of money. These were two-reeler shorts, filmed by people who didn't even want to pay the creator a royalty. But at least Mother and I were no longer downright poor. We moved into a small, comfortable house in a quiet, unfashionable neighborhood a few miles to the east of Hollywood. My time was split between making McGuire movies and going to school.

Whenever I headed for school, my mother gave me twenty-five cents as lunch money. Now that there was ample food, meals had become less important to me. But words were interesting. With my quarters I organized a kind of private language seminar.

The grade school had a varied assortment of pupils from mostly poor homes. I, with the quarter, was a capitalist. Each day I'd round up three boys, one Italian, one Japanese, one Chinese, and pay them a penny for every word they could teach me in their own language. *La Dolce Vita*, for example, was worth three cents at the going rates. (I didn't like the picture, either.) *Sayonara* was a hard-earned penny for the Japanese kid. The Chinese boy? Well, we did our work in a yard sitting under a *ku-tu shu-mu*, which means solitary tree.

The language seminar lasted only until my mother noticed that I seemed to be starving every afternoon at four o'clock. She investigated. My school of languages went out of business forever.

The McGuire movies didn't make me a hot property, in the sense that Jackie Cooper became a hot property as soon as he made *his* picture about a comic strip character. Jackie's picture was called *Skippy*, and it was such a smash that Louis B. Mayer not only signed Jack to a rich contract at MGM, he took him on a yacht trip to Santa Catalina Island, along with Tallulah Bankhead and Joan Crawford, who were there to row in case anything went wrong with Mr. Mayer's engines.

My career didn't explode into opulence, as Jackie's and Shirley Temple's did. It was a long time before I was truly established. But then my career didn't suddenly disappear, either. Jackie went into a slump after a director

noticed hair on his legs and made him shave. Some say
Shirley Temple was never the same after she bought her
first brassiere. My career, which started more slowly, was
more enduring. I didn't get into trouble until the late
1940's, when I was pushing thirty.

Ripening slowly, as a grape in the shade, I was just
promising enough to attract an agent. His name was
Harry Weber, and he was an honest man. My mother had
known Harry slightly in New York and now he was in
Hollywood, a specialist in handling child actors.

"Your boy can do more things than Mickey McGuire,"
he said.

I wondered what he meant by that remark, and spent
the next few years finding out.

The very distant movies blur a little, there were so
many of them. *Not to Be Trusted*, with Mat Moore
and Bud Jamison. Something called *My Pal, The King*,
with Tom Mix. Ten days' work for me. Two hundred and
fifty dollars. In something else, called *Orchids and Ermine*, I got away from playing the child. I played a
midget. Now this midget was a big hogman from Walla
Walla, Washington. In one scene, Colleen Moore, one of
the brightest stars of that era, was seated behind a desk as
I approached. All she saw was just a cane on which was
perched a hat. It was some time before she saw me.
Funny, I suppose, but visual.

There was one bad moment on the set of *Orchids and
Ermine*. A baby tooth popped right out of my mouth.
Here was the great big midget of a hogman from Walla

Walla, forty if he was a day, missing a tooth and looking like a little boy. My mother solved the problem. She retrieved the tooth and secured it into place with a piece of chewing gum. The child was a midget again. Cameras could roll. So long as I moved my tongue cautiously, the day was saved.

I don't remember a hell of a lot about the early pictures and neither does anyone else. Some titles stick in my head: *Fast Companions, The Big Cage, The Life of Jimmy Dolan, Broadway to Hollywood, The Big Chance, The Chief.* Keep watching *The Late, Late, Late Show* and maybe you'll see one. If the celluloid hasn't turned to dust.

I think it was Larry Darmour who suggested that my name be changed to Mickey McGuire. At least, it was Darmour who was paying the royalty to Fontaine Fox. Actually, I'd become so identified with the McGuire character that most of the children I played with had been calling me "Mickey" anyway. The shorts were in all the movie houses and when the kids I knew went to the movies on Saturday, there I was on the screen—not Joe Yule, nor Sonny, but Mickey. I guess even then I was better on film than in real life. Anyway, the children called me Mickey.

As soon as Darmour had my name changed legally I understand he cut Fox off from the thousand-dollar royalty. As soon as Fox was cut off, he brought suit against Darmour, the studio, everyone. The suit dragged on for a long time and I don't know what the judge did about Fox. Saw that he got some satisfaction, I believe.

All the kids liked the Mickey McGuire character, although I had to take some good-natured razzing. (There was never any touch of bitterness or jealousy from the gang. It seems I had to become an adult to first encounter jealousy, intrigue and designed deceit.)

But Mickey McGuire, like childhood itself, was destined to end. My ability to comprehend the McGuire scripts and deliver the job brought me to the attention of the controlling people at Universal Studios. They wanted a child actor—me—but they felt that they didn't want the association with my previous acting in the short subjects. Thus, when that studio offered me employment, it appeared that a new name was a necessity. Joe Yule, Jr., was no more, and Mickey McGuire was going—but I was still Mickey. There was a publicity man at Universal who said he thought that the name Mickey Rooney had a nice sound to it. Everyone else thought so, too. It certainly sounded better than Mickey Yule or Joe McGuire. So that in fact, not fiction, is how I came to be known as Mickey Rooney. Later we had my name legally changed for good. So my very name is the product of publicity.

My schooling through these working years was never intensive and my approach to books was never dedicated. In the first days of the *Mickey McGuire* series, there was time enough for me to attend a public elementary school. I was quick if not thorough, glib if not thoughtful, and I got by without much difficulty and without much learning. Just as I could remember lines and memorize songs from my earliest days, so I could remember school work when I had to. I'd remember a script for the length of a picture, say two or three weeks. I'd remember my school work even more briefly, just till the next exam.

Later, I was wrapped up in too many different projects to attend a public school and my mother enrolled me in Ma Lawlor's, a school for professional children. I'll say this for Ma Lawlor's: no child ever broke down under the study load. But since I was appearing in pictures, and taking dancing lessons on the side, Ma Lawlor's approach was probably just as well.

Instruction at Ma Lawlor's proceeded at a leisurely pace and there was plenty of time to get to know the other pupils. One girl I met there will be more important to my story as it progresses. When I first met her, her name was Frances Gumm and she was one of the Singing Gumm Sisters. When I first worked in a movie with her, her name, like mine, had undergone surgery. Out of the anesthesia, she became Judy Garland.

II

Everyone probably has a fictional hero; everyone, that is, who reads. Mine isn't, as for some others, Hamlet. Nor is he Ulysses, nor David Copperfield, nor (forgive me) Andy Hardy. My fictional hero is Robin Goodfellow, alias Puck.

The line on the Frontpiece bears repeating here:

How now, spirit! whither wander you?

Puck says that in *A Midsummer Night's Dream*. In fact, it is the first thing he says. Like so much in Shakespeare these few words establish a tone which is mysterious, compelling and correct.

Puck, the comic, the supernatural, speeding through the night on an impish errand, but in the end a gentle being, gentle Puck.

Puck, who speaks with striking cogency, as, "I'll put a girdle round the earth in forty minutes," or, "What fools these mortals be."

Puck, who transforms the head of a bad actor into the head of an ass, thereby finishing what the actor had begun.

Puck, whose character has given a word to the language.

Puck, who observes "those things best do please me that befall preposterously."

Puck, who for all his wild and strident laughter, would make a world in which:

> *Jack shall have Jill;*
> *Nought shall go ill;*
> *The man shall have his mare again,*
> *And all shall be well.*

A world that we would all like to make—Puck's world, clear as a sunburst through all the wild laughter.

I was introduced to Puck almost a quarter of a century ago by a man who spoke no English. His name was Max Reinhardt. He was a great German director who hap-

pened to be Jewish so that, at the suggestion of the
management, he left his native country. He came to California to produce and direct *A Midsummer Night's Dream*
as a play in Hollywood Bowl, that vast open-air theater
set amid spiny grassless hills.

Before Shakespeare, I had appeared in *Lost Jungle*,
Beloved and a few other similar classics of the silver-
plated screen. I don't remember the directors I'd worked
for. I could laugh on cue and cry on cue and I always
knew my lines so they pretty much left me alone. At the
time I was neither a student of the theater nor an admirer
of directors. But even I had heard of Max Reinhardt.

The community of Hollywood was vastly excited at the
first hint that he might be coming, for Max Reinhardt had
done superb things in the European theater, things that
were at once imaginative and daring, and if there were
two things Hollywood wasn't in 1934, those were it.
Imaginative and daring. In making motion pictures, I
mean. Naturally, people admire someone with more courage than they. Reinhardt was a hero before he got off the
train. He was also a most familiar business reference.

As Jews of the German theater fled before Hitler, many
of them came to Hollywood with talent, without much
money, and with a message. "Call Ernst Lubitsch," Reinhardt, who was still in Germany, had told them, "He will
help you."

So they came and when they came they called Lubitsch, a fine comic director. One caller was Max Reinhardt's nephew. Another was Max Reinhardt's cousin. A
third was a pupil. A fourth was an assistant. Finally there

came a day when Gottfried Reinhardt came to Hollywood and, following instructions, telephoned Lubitsch.

"Who's calling?" Lubitsch's secretary asked.

"Max Reinhardt's son," Gottfried Reinhardt said.

The secretary hung up. I think Gottfried had to produce his birth certificate before Lubitsch would believe him.

When Reinhardt announced that he would audition for *A Midsummer Night's Dream,* actors raced down from the hills. There was not much money to be made appearing in the play, but appearing for Reinhardt was first a great honor and second a matter of status. Or first a matter of status and second a great honor. It all depended on the actor.

Olivia de Haviland wanted to play Puck. Although Puck is male, Olivia was only eighteen years old and, in proper costuming, could have passed for a boy. Mary Pickford wanted to play Puck. She was forty years old, but still slim. I was signed to play Puck. Me. Mickey (Himself) Rooney, aged thirteen.

People, critics among them, have praised my work in Reinhardt's movie of *A Midsummer Night's Dream.* I think their praise is misdirected for reasons I'll explain presently. But in Reinhardt's play of *A Midsummer Night's Dream,* I was about as good as I ever get.

How can a thirteen-year-old play Shakespeare? Or, more correctly, how can a thirteen-year-old who has never previously read Shakespeare play Shakespeare? There is no precise answer. Something in the wild and gentle Puck struck a chord of understanding within me, within a youth who if not yet wild, was no longer truly gentle. Some vitality Shakespeare had infused into a character four centuries earlier stirred a corresponding vitality in me. It is a wonder of the theater that Puck, conceived by a young writer, perhaps as he sipped dry sherry in some forgotten London tavern, should live in another time in the mind of a boy living amid the reclaimed desert that is Los Angeles. It is a wonder, and beyond explanation. I have played a Rod Serling character well and I can understand some of the reasons why I did. With Shakespeare's character, I only play the role. I cannot understand why I *can* play it any more than I can understand the genius that was William Shakespeare.

"Read the part carefully," people told me before the audition. "Read it slowly. Shakespeare is pretty complicated stuff."

Shakespeare in general may be, but to my young eyes, Puck was not. As I turned the pages of the script, he came alive. Almost as quickly as I read the lines, I remembered them. When it seemed right for Puck to laugh, I laughed. But the laugh was not my own. It was Puck's laugh—part the mocking bray of a donkey, part the overflowing laughter of a child. Quickly, inexplicably, a character had been born. When it came time to recite, I recited well. Then I laughed Puck's laugh and Reinhardt hired me.

His direction was serious, involved and German. Almost everything he said was in German, but he had an associate named Felix Weissberger, who translated. At one point, Puck, speaking disdainfully of mortals, says:

> *Up and down, up and down;*
> *I will lead them up and down:*
> *I am fear'd in field and town;*
> *Goblin, lead them up and down.*

Here, Reinhardt explained through Weissberger, I was to use my whole body as I said the lines. I was actually to bounce up and down as I said "up and down." This was a tiny detail, one of perhaps a hundred tiny details, that in sum made for an excellent performance. Although I had been onstage for more than eleven years, Reinhardt's was the first outstanding direction ever given me. I honestly don't believe I have since worked for a comparably outstanding director. Not one. If I had, I would be a better actor today.

My costume, as Puck, could barely fill a thimble. I wore something like a loincloth and underneath that an athletic supporter. As a baby, I had gotten into difficulty talking about athletic supporters. Now, at dress rehearsal, I got into difficulty wearing one.

Early in the second act, Oberon, who is kind of the supernatural character in the play, commands: "My gentle Puck, come hither."

As Reinhardt organized the scene, I was concealed in the branches of a real tree. At the words "come hither," I was to drop lightly to the stage in front of Oberon.

"My gentle Puck, come hither," Oberon said.

I tried to drop from the tree with no success.

"My gentle Puck, come hither," Oberon repeated.

The tree held me as though it were an octopus.

"I can't come hither," said gentle Puck, "my leotard is hooked around a branch." My face was not the only thing that was bare.

Weissberger translated and even The Great Reinhardt laughed.

A *Midsummer Night's Dream* ran for a month at the Hollywood Bowl. It was so successful that Warner Brothers decided to make the play into a movie, the first time, I think, that a studio did battle with William Shakespeare. I say battle quite seriously. As I recall the screen credits, there was one line that said "written by William Shakespeare." Then there was another line that said "additional dialogue by . . ." Well, I forget the writer. Where but in Hollywood would someone be assigned to improve on Shakespeare?

("Now look, Havenhurst, we got this Limey play that we're stuck doing and I want you to jazz it up a little. Fix it, know what I mean? Be a play doctor like George S. Kaufman. I got the thing somewhere on the bookshelf here . . . among these volumes . . . Let's see. *Ruined Women Tell Their Stories. Sex for Two. Vitamins and Virility.* Oh, here it is. *Shakespeare, W., Collected Plays.*")

In most standard movie contracts, there is a clause which limits an actor's conduct in three areas:

1. He may not get drunk.
2. He may not commit adultery.
3. He must pay his taxes.

People have maintained that if all three provisions were enforced rigidly, no one could ever make a movie.

At the time of *Midsummer Night* contracts, I was a little young for booze. I was interested in girls but still no major threat. But I was not without vices real or imagined. In the imagination of the studio, my major vice was sports.

Table tennis was my specialty; I got good enough to play in the finals of the California Junior Championships. I suppose ping-pong is risky. You can develop a hangnail putting a top spin on your serve. I also liked football, baseball and diving. In the studio's view, football meant a shattered knee, baseball meant a fractured skull and diving meant death by drowning. I was a teen-age boy with a normal teen-age interest in sports, but I was also a teen-age investment. The studio didn't want its investment running end or doing jackknives, so someone inserted a special clause in my contract. It had nothing to do with wine, women or taxes. It simply forbade me from participating in sports.

The psychology was absurd. Tell a teen-ager he can't shoot craps and, even if he's never handled dice before, he'll damn well get himself into a game. Order a teen-ager to stay away from a girl, and he'll end up in a paternity suit (if he has the right, or wrong, girl). Tell a teen-ager to mind his manners, and you have a movie title. *I Was a Teen-Age Werewolf* is the title that comes to mind.

As soon as I discovered that I was not allowed to participate in sports, my interest, which had been strong, became fanatic. I kept after my mother to let me play this, let me play that, and after a while I broke down her resistance. "We'll go up to Big Bear Mountain," she said. "If you have to roughhouse, at least do it in the snow." The snow, she reasoned, was soft and therefore safe.

In Southern California, you can drive from summer to winter in a few hours. When we got to Big Bear, I wandered off, looking for something exciting. I found something exciting soon enough, under a sign that read, To-BOGGANS FOR HIRE. I rented one and recruited three or four older boys to ride it with me. The more weight in a toboggan, the faster it goes, and I wanted to go fast. I took the front position and we set off down the mountain. We went fast, all right, and we were still going fast when the toboggan crashed into a tree.

Cries. A tangle of bodies. Unbelievable pain. I was lying in the snow with one leg twisted on top of me so that it was almost resting on my face. It was my own leg that was twisted. I couldn't stand the leg that way. I couldn't stand the sight of the deformity. I grabbed the pants and all but hurled the leg into a normal position. Then, very quickly, there was another sled and people were trying to give me first aid. They put my leg in traction, and lifted me onto the second sled and took me down to the bottom of the mountain. I went back to Los Angeles strapped to a toboggan on the rear seat of a car. The ride took eight hours. The leg was broken. Badly. Specifically, I had broken the bone between the thigh and knee called the femur. The doctors told me two things that I had not guessed. If the leg hadn't broken as it did, the crash and the weight of those bodies behind me would have split me clear up the middle. Alas poor Yorick. Then, somehow, in hurling the broken leg away from my face I had placed the bone fragments in excellent position for resetting.

Did you ever break your leg, Mr. Rooney?

Sure, and I set the bone myself.

I played Puck, in the movie, on one leg. For the "up and down" scene, they had to build a special platform with a hole in it. I stuck the cast into the hole and went up and down with a maneuver something like a knee bend. On one knee. That cast is why I wasn't satisfied with myself as Puck in the movie. Still, I realize that for all its hobbled imperfections my work as Puck, more than any other single role up to that time, established me.

III

I could feel great days coming. In my early teens, I knew. Hell, I could act and dance and play the drums and I could almost see that jackpot ahead of me. I wanted to do everything, be everything, try everything. Acting wasn't work; it was delight. And I could make money at it, make money doing the thing that I liked best. By the time I played in A Midsummer Night's Dream I was earning about $500 a week. This was in mid-depression. Taxes were low. It wasn't a fortune, but it was a helluva lot, and there was more coming for sure. I was only beginning. I was young and I was tough. If I had to, I could make all the money in the world.

Thus one seed of trouble was sown. I've never been interested in money. I'm interested in things that money can buy, but that's different. I get no kick out of amassing capital, clipping coupons, surveying holdings. I mean I didn't when I had holdings to survey. Budgets? Pension plans? Investment programs? The hell with them. I'm an actor, not a businessman. (You fool.)

Those early years of near poverty didn't scare me. I was too young to know that we were poor. Then, as I grew old enough to want things, I began to make money. Maybe $75 a week for the first *Mickey McGuire* pictures. Then $100. Then $150. Elevator going up. Whenever I wanted more things, I could make more money to buy them. Money was like air. It wasn't something to think about. It was there.

My mother did her best to counsel me. But how much counsel could she give? Ten years before, she had been making $25 a week—during those weeks when she worked. Studio people? They were interested in me as a property here and now. MGM wasn't running a child guidance clinic. Get out there, kid, and give 'em hell, and there'll be plenty more where that last check came from. Agents? Agents are going to have a chapter all to themselves.

So there was all this make-believe money around me, only it wasn't make-believe money, it was real. What was there to do with it? I knew plenty about baseball and football when I was thirteen. I also knew about horse racing. While lying in bed in that hospital, with my broken leg in a cast, I was bored and, as always, restless. I read *Variety* because I was in show business, and I read the *Racing Form,* because there was all that make-believe money to burn and all that time to kill. Lying in bed, I started quoting the *Form* to doctors and nurses. A few of them read the *Form* themselves. A few more became interested and wanted to bet.

"I'll book your bets," I offered.

As a thirteen-year-old, recuperating from a fractured leg in a hospital, I ran my own bookmaking service. Everyone thought it was cute, losers excepted.

I wish often and profoundly that someone had clutched me by one ear, taken me aside and lectured, saying, "Maybe you're good, but you're lucky, too, and luck doesn't last forever. It's no crime to be a businessman. It's not wrong to take time off once in a while to consider where all the money is coming from, where it's going, what might happen if the money stops. But nobody told me and I didn't stop to think. I was the Monopoly Money Kid. It was only years later, when I failed at marriage and a lot of other important things, that I realized the Monopoly Money had been real.

Everything was breathless in those days. I can—I don't know why—turn on an emotion the way you turn on a faucet. I can laugh and gag immediately before a poignant, moving scene and, as soon as the director calls "Roll 'em," break into tears with no period of transition. Or it can be the other way. I can feel low, depressed and troubled, just before a comic scene, and switch to laughter in an instant. Then, when the scene ends and the laughter stops, I find myself as depressed as I'd been going in. Turning on emotion is some kind of knack. Take it and add to it my ability to memorize quickly and you've explained why acting isn't work to me.

Some cheerful child actors have to be abused before playing sad scenes. Directors shout at them, threaten them, steal their candy before these children manage to cry. As a result, the kids are emotionally spent after a day before the cameras. I never was, never am. Breathless is the word. Read the *Racing Form* in a dressing room. Start to write a song. Go out and start to cry on cue. Wipe tears. Go back and finish song. Gimme Blue Beetle in the seventh. Gimme a diminished fifth.

After Shakespeare, I was offered several strong roles at MGM. There was *Ah, Wilderness!*, the only comedy Eugene O'Neill ever wrote. From burlesque to Shakespeare and O'Neill in a decade, I would have told myself had I bothered to stop and think and tell myself anything, which I didn't.

Then there was a movie called *Riff-Raff*, in which I worked with Spencer Tracy and Jean Harlow. I played a tough kid. Type casting. For one scene, I was supposed to walk on a roof ledge about thirty feet above the ground, a bit that unnerved everyone but me.

"We'll use a double here, Mick," the director said.

"The hell you will," I said.

"Now look, Mickey, there's no sense in taking unnecessary chances. A double will walk on the ledge."

"Please let me do it."

I was fourteen. I could do anything. I walked the ledge myself, after a wire was attached to my waist, a wire strong enough to support me if I fell, but too thin to show up on film. I walked the ledge easily, without stumbling.

It was on this, the set of *Riff-Raff*, that I became friendly with someone who has been close to me for almost thirty years. His name is Sig Frohlich and probably you've never heard of him. He is an actor—he's also been a stunt man—and he is one of the legion of almost anonymous people without whom the movie business could not function.

Sig was a boy from the lower East Side of New York. He had traveled to Hollywood because he found there wasn't much doing in New York. If nothing else, Hollywood was a different place. Sig had no prospects, no deals ahead of him. Like thousands of others during the depression, he went west on impulse.

My toboggan adventure had convinced the studio that if there was anything more dangerous than my participating in sports, it was a contract forbidding me from participating in sports. So, sadly, they conceded that as long as I was a teen-ager, I was going to act like a teen-ager. (Actually, I acted like a teen-ager into my thirties.) If I wanted to play a little touch football, there might not be any harm in that. If I insisted on playing a little baseball, all right. Just stay away from mountains, will ya?

I got to know Sig well on a touch football team I organized in a prairie on the lot. As I say, he was a tough kid from New York. I was a tough kid from all over. We hit it off then; we liked the same things. Sig was a little older and in later years he was to perform such acts of friendship as telling me off when I was wrong and not leaving me when everyone did. We've been friends for a long time. Sig is stuck with me—our love for each other is as strong as that of brothers.

I wasn't going to be the tallest man in the world. I realized that in my early teens. I wanted to be taller, the way every boy wants to be taller, but it didn't shake me, didn't throw me, didn't change my personality.

I was a kid on the rise with everything in the world ahead of him. A kid who could do a lot of things. I was a kid who had money and was going to have more. I was also a kid who stood five foot three when the bones stopped growing.

I went to three different high schools. One was Fairfax High, which (surprise) is in the Fairfax section of Los Angeles. Another was Hollywood High, which sits right on Sunset Boulevard. The third was Ma Lawlor's, a school which not only went easy on actors of grade school age, but went easy on actors of high school age, too.

In Fairfax I found some friends, briefly. I don't remember who they were. I don't remember their names. Like many of the ships that passed in my particular dawn, they soon went out of sight.

At Ma Lawlor's there was Judy, and Sidney Miller, who now has become a director of note, and a number of other professional children. I still see Sidney.

At Hollywood High, or in a malted milk shop across the

street from Hollywood High, I first met Judy Turner (later Lana). I think I was seventeen. Judy was a year younger, chronologically. The first time I saw her, I saw what millions of people were later to see: poise, a superb figure, and that beautiful, innocent, know-it-all face. My eyes bugged, and not my eyes alone. Lana Turner, at sixteen, was the belle of Hollywood High.

The malt shop was a social club; everyone congregated there, including Lana. In fact, when Lana was there, everyone congregated around Lana.

Jackie Cooper, who had been dating Lana, claims that I took her away from him because I got a driver's license first, and Lana liked to travel in style. This is nonsense. I took her away from him, but the license had nothing to do with it. Class, it was. Sheer class.

I dated Lana for three or four months. Movies, dancing, dinners. Then I guess my class ran out. She was climbing onward and upward, and part of that climb meant more mature men. There was no stopping Turner. I knew that long ago, just as I knew there was no stopping Rooney. Lana was going to make it big, although she wasn't much at acting at the time.

What was it like dating Lana Turner when I was seventeen years old? Did you ever date the prettiest girl in school when you were seventeen years old? And did you find out that she was as warm and as sophisticated as she was pretty? Congratulations. Now you know what it would have been like to date Lana Turner when you were seventeen years old. For further detail, I suggest you consult the lady.

A car, of course, was important. I forget whether I was

sixteen or seventeen when I got my first, a bright blue Ford convertible. I was working on the day when my junior driver's license came through and I asked Sig Frohlich to pick up the car. Sig, it turned out, didn't have a license of his own, and he had to send someone else to pick it up. Anyway, an emissary of an emissary brought back the Ford convertible, and I was off. I drove it hard to see how quickly it would roll from a standing start. I drove it hard to see how fast it would go. I was a hard driver. Now, however, I've changed my ways. I never go faster than sixty miles an hour. Sixty on the highway, sixty on the streets, but never more than sixty.

Would you like to know a pleasant sensation? Drive your first car fast down an open road with the top down, and Lana Turner sitting beside you, holding on and urging you to go slower. At least, that was my idea of a pleasant sensation. It might not have been Lana's.

In 1936, I made *The Devil Is a Sissy* and *Little Lord Fauntleroy*. Freddie Bartholomew was the little lord himself.

I was getting hotter. The end of the contract I had signed with Metro was in sight. Agents talked with Louis B. Mayer, or Louis B. Mayer talked to agents and then one day I was running to Sig with the good news. "Guess what! I've got to go to court. I'm signing a new contract." Those were *happy* court days.

There was a fairly new law in California, called the Coogan Law after Jackie Coogan, which specified that no child actor could be signed to a contract without the approval of a judge. It also stipulated that a good chunk of the child's earnings had to go into a trust. A good thing, but still no protection against myself. When trust money comes due now, I never see it. The money goes directly from trust to District Director of Internal Revenue. Want to know an unpleasant sensation? Get behind on your income tax.

My mother remarried in 1937. Her groom was Fred Pankey, a graduate of Knox College, who was an accountant and was, in later years, a solitary voice, urging me not to make some of the mistakes that I insisted on making. I liked Fred. He was a big, handsome man, possessed of a fine intelligence, who took upon himself the role of the heavy. By that I mean, he tried to warn me that a day might come when the money would stop. Under some circumstances, he might have had a chance. But not after I looked at the new contract.

It called for a starting base of $750 a week. Then $1,250. Then $1,500. Then $2,500. A week that is. Plus bonuses.

By way of celebration, we bought a house on Densmore, in Encino, which is in the San Fernando Valley. I'll tell you about that house, my house, the first home for which I felt real pride. It sat on five acres and there was a pool, and there were English walnut trees, and lemon trees and forests of gardenias and nine telephones and sterling silver fixtures in the bathrooms. The house was built of stone and had twelve rooms or more, and it cost $75,000. It seems lavish, but it really wasn't. Not by the standards of Hollywood in those days.

I didn't build something like Valentino's Falcon's Lair, or Mary Pickford's Pickfair. We bought a hell of a house, but we didn't buy it in Beverly Hills. To get from Encino to what were supposed to be the more fashionable towns, you have to drive across one of the canyons that cuts through the Hollywood Hills. The difference in price between houses on one side of the Hills and the other is like the difference between apartments on the East Side of Manhattan and apartments in Bayonne, New Jersey.

What we did was buy a comfortable house—maybe a little more than comfortable—in an area where the prices, judged against my salary, weren't outlandish. Later the studio had some postcards printed with a picture of my home and a label: MICKEY ROONEY'S HOUSE. Years later, when I went to a party thrown by some sponsors of a television show, I saw a house that really belonged on a postcard. Compared to that, my Densmore House was a garage—a garage for a Rolls-Royce, maybe, but still a garage.

We paid only $5,000 down. In those days, I was a great credit risk. There were payments to be made every six months and we made them. Eventually we owned the place free and clear. In fact, we owned it free and clear just in time to sell it. But from 1937 through 1947, through two marriages and I don't know how many parties, the Densmore place was my home.

The house is still where it was, but the grounds are gone. It makes me feel a little sad when I drive past. Some developer has put up 2,000 ranch houses in what used to be my backyard and the surrounding hills.

4 * *The First*
Million Dollars

I

Overall, the Andy Hardy movies grossed $75 million, of which a small but significant fraction was paid to me.

No one expected Andy Hardy to become a Comstock Lode. No one expected him to become a temporary Tom Sawyer. No one expected him to do anything but make a small profit and, like ten thousand other movie characters, fade away with next week's change of bill. Andy surprised everyone including myself. He first appeared in the 1937 picture *A Family Affair*, and, unlike his portrayer, he jes' growed.

Bingo. Bank night. Jackpot. Yes, it's thank you, Mr. Rooney *and* the bands begin to play. Hello, America. Good morning, America. Yes, it's true, America. I'm for real.

During the late 1930's, Metro-Goldwyn-Mayer was geared to a schedule of fifty-two pictures a year, one movie a week. There were sets by the acre, directors by the dozen, writers by the score and, the studio advertised, "more stars than there are in the heavens." Louis B. Mayer, a bespectacled, short-tempered emperor, presided and for several years earned the highest salary of anyone in the United States. (Of course assorted Rockefellers and Fords grossed more, but Mayer's was the highest straight salary.)

Privately, Mr. Mayer refused to assume the role of monk, but in his pictures, he stood four square behind purity, virtue, and virginity. He liked movies about mothers (provided the mothers did not have sons named Oedipus). He liked movies about horses (provided the animals were free of hoof-and-mouth disease and closed fast in the final eighth). He liked movies about physicians (provided the doctors undercharged their patients). And he liked movies about growing boys (provided the boys did not radiate, in even a minor form, any degree of delinquency).

Mayer's private life wasn't my concern. It was his own business. But publicly, he favored an almost puritanical morality which invaded all of his pictures. He did not like complicated movies, controversial movies, arty movies, political movies, nor even blatantly sexual movies. I am not saying that he had Lana Turner outfitted in the concealing breastplates of a fourteenth-century knight. Turner's bosom was an important corporate asset. But the bosom, in the pictures, was a kind of a prop. Sex began with a gentle kiss on the cheek and ended with an intense kiss on the mouth. It never went further.

The policy of public prudery was not the result of pressure groups forcing Mayer to make movies which were "wholesome," or wholesomer than thou. Mr. Mayer made wholesome super-American movies because that was how he thought movies should be made. If there was one persistent message it was this: Everybody, except the heavies, falls in love, has some struggles and finally ends up with the Right One. The name of the game was a four-letter word. Love. Take away love stories—puppy love, young love, mature love, love through a lifetime—and MGM would have had to go into the newsreel business.

It is easy now to look back at the late 1930's, when Hitler was holding hands with Stalin and the old world was dying, and wonder where Mr. Mayer thought he was going with this endless train of relatively unimportant love stories. If Mayer were still alive, he would answer with something like: "Movies should be about beautiful people doing beautiful things. That's what the public wants. Don't bother me with politics, sadism, gut-bucket sex or VD."

MGM was this vast factory, the General Motors of the movie business, dedicated to Mr. Mayer's views of morality, and to mass entertainment. For along with his public view of virtue, Mayer believed, publicly, privately, profoundly, in profit. To him, movies were a mass medium, and filling the numberless theaters that played MGM pictures was the height of his art. You made nice clean movies because that was the right thing to do, and you kept them simple because that was what the public wanted. Cleanliness plus simplicity equaled box office.

Currently, Hollywood is on a binge of superrealistic super-sexy pictures. Why? Because these days superrealistic, super-sexy pictures make money. It is, generally, a bad time for illusions. We used to have the illusion of the great star, someone who was remote, someone who was oddly different from ourselves. He, or she, was glamour. The illusion of the star was a big thing in Hollywood. Look at TV today. There's the great Harry James. He's playing Kleenex. There's the great Edward G. Robinson. He's out in the kitchen making Maxwell House Coffee.

The themes in the movie business today are supposed to be "adult." I think it was the other night I saw this "adult" picture. Seems there was this unwed mother, hooked on dope, who was in love with her sister. Maybe you saw it, too.

Next week we'll probably find out that all these years Trigger has hated Roy Rogers.

Anyway, the reason there's so much sex in movies today comes down to two words: box office.

If the day comes when sex ceases to be box office, those daring, audacious, shocking movies we see advertised will disappear. If sex ceases to be box office. . . . Forget the premise. I'm just making a point.

As Mayer saw it and as almost everyone has seen it since, we are in the movie *business,* the movie industry. You can paint a picture with a sheet of canvas and a few dollars' worth of oils. You can write a poem with one piece of paper and last year's stubby pencil. Provided you are sufficiently talented, both are art. Movies, in the hands of a few gifted people, can become art, but no matter how they end, they always begin with the need for cold cash. Somebody has to hire a writer. Good movie writers come high. Say $40,000 and a percentage of the gross, and up. Maybe the movie starts with the purchase of rights to a novel or a play. That can run $100,000 and much more. Now you have a story and a writer—you've begun—and you're out $140,000. Then there are actors to be hired and, in our strange society, skilled actors make fifty times as much as skilled teachers. The actors will perform on sets, which means that carpenters are needed. The sets must be lighted. That means electricians. Then there's a director and a producer, and an assistant director and an assistant producer, and makeup men and costumers, and assistant makeup men and assistant costumers and relatives—the list could run through this page and the next. Before the first scene is filmed, a legion has been hired. If it's a Roman epic, two legions, not counting the slave girls.

These days most movies are made as individual efforts—I'll go into that later. But during the days of Andy Hardy, almost all movies were produced by studios. Metro had an immense investment—as well as immense pride—in its staffs of writers, actors, directors, technicians and workmen. It was geared to turn out fifty-two pictures a year, because that was what was needed to keep the caldrons bubbling and to make sure that everyone got paid.

In the year 1937, I appeared in six pictures. I believe *A Family Affair* was the second one. The others were *Cap-*

*tains Courageous, The Hoosier Schoolboy, Thorough-
breds Don't Cry, Live, Love and Dream,* and *Slave Ship.* I
was hot and they were working me. In 1938, when I was
even hotter, I made nine pictures. Three were Andy
Hardys. We were turning out mass entertainment and we
were turning it out fast, but in good taste.

Andy Hardy was a phenomenon. He wasn't handsome,
because I wasn't. He wasn't any bigger than I, either. But
somehow he struck an image that flared all across the
country among young people who told themselves, "I'm
like that," and among parents who said, "Hey, that's my
boy." Andy was a super-typical young man who lived in a
super-typical small town called Carvel. He had both
schemes and dreams, which always caused complications
a few minutes into the picture and always produced
general happiness at the end. Andy had a sister, with
whom he squabbled about the use of the telephone, plus
dates who were to include Lana Turner, Esther Williams,
Kathryn Grayson, Donna Reed, Judy Garland and Ann
Rutherford. He had a father who was a small-town judge
as honest as Abe Lincoln, and a mother who was as sweet
as my own. (The Hardy family was so *clean* Andy only
shook hands with her.)

People believed in Andy with a dedicated naïveté.
Katherine Brush, who wrote the novel *Young Man of
Manhattan,* and later a Hardy script, once pointed out:
"Because the movie public knows the Hardys like neigh-
bors, the writer has to spend days soaking in preliminary
information—such things as the genealogy of the Hardy
family for three generations back. . . . Infinite pains are

taken to keep the family precisely average, lest parents protest that Andy is setting a bad example. Once he was made to say about a meal cooked by his mother, 'This dinner's no good, Mom.' There had to be a retake in which he said, 'It was a fine dinner, Mom. A lovely dinner. But I just wasn't hungry.' "

Metro was not setting out to create a national figure when they cast me as Andy Hardy. They wanted a quick, successful picture, one out of fifty-two, cheaper than the big spectaculars, more expensive than the quickest quickies. In short, it was a typical picture that originated typical Andy Hardy.

When the public reaction to Andy, by mail, by phone, by wire and by box office receipts, turned out to be so strong, MGM, like General Motors with a hot new car, was perfectly equipped to roll. They had writers ready to pound out scripts, directors ready to plan camera angles, press agents ready to promote. And, happily, they had girls.

As the Hardy series developed in 1937, '38 and '39, the character of Andy expanded and deepened somewhat. During these years, which took me from the age of sixteen past my twentieth birthday, my own character expanded somewhat, too. But there was no connection between what you saw of Andy Hardy on the screen and what was the reality of Mickey Rooney off camera.

The key to Andy's development was a series of man-to-man talks he held with his father, the courtly, conservative Judge, played by the courtly, dashing Lewis Stone.

Mickey Rooney, two years old

Mickey Maguire series

Mickey as Puck in *Midsummer Night's Dream*

eft to right: Freddie Bartholomew, Ann Gillis, Mickey, Deanna Durbin, Judy arland, Jackie Cooper

Shirley Temple, Judy Garland, Mickey, Louis B. Mayer

Clark Gable, Shirley Temple, Mickey, Judy Garland

Mickey and Judy Garland

Spencer Tracy and Mickey in
Boys' Town

Mickey and Wallace Beery in *Slave Ship*

Left: Mickey and father, Joe Yule, Jr. *Right:* Mickey and Elizabeth Taylor in *National Velvet*

Left: Mickey and Esther Williams in *Love Comes to Andy Hardy. Right:* Mickey and Judy Garland in *Words and Music*

Standing: Mickey Rooney, Jr.; Tim Rooney
Front row: Kelly Ann, Barbara, Mickey, Kyle
In pool: Kerry

Kerry, Mickey, Kelly Ann (*seated in front*), Kyle and Barbara

Mickey in *Requiem for a Heavyweight*

Mickey with his sons Timmy and Junior

Once Andy signed a note to buy a car on time. Of course, he couldn't make the payments and the auto dealer threatened to take him to court. Rather than face his father across the judge's bench, Andy confessed in the living room of the Hardy household. The dialogue then went something like this:

JUDGE HARDY: A promissory note is a solemn responsibility, Andy.

ANDY (*with trembling lower lip*): I know that, Dad.

JUDGE: Weren't you aware of it at the time you signed it?

ANDY: I guess I wasn't, really.

JUDGE: Well, perhaps this can be a lesson to you, Andy. Perhaps in the future you'll understand that you must never enter into an obligation unless you are quite certain you can honor it. Is that clear, Andy?

ANDY: Yes, Dad.

JUDGE: How much do you owe that auto dealer?

ANDY (*near tears*): Seven dollars.

JUDGE: We may be able to devise some means for me to advance the money, and for you to work off your debt to me over the next few months.

That was Andy Hardy—working off a seven-dollar debt over months. Mickey Rooney? He was making more than seven dollars a minute.

Often Andy had trouble with a girl. Then there would be man-to-man talks along these lines:

ANDY: Well, it's all over, Dad. I'm a failure. I'm not worth anything, to you or anybody else. I'm going away, but don't worry about me, Dad. I'll be all right.

JUDGE HARDY: This wouldn't have anything to do with a certain new young lady in town, would it, Andy?

ANDY: I'm through with women, Dad.

JUDGE (*grinning a little*): You know, long ago, Andy, I was interested in girls, too.

ANDY (*shocked*): You were?

JUDGE: And once, before I met your mother, there was a new young lady in town and I thought that she was quite a lovely person. Then we had a falling out and it turned out to be the most fortunate thing that ever happened to me.

ANDY: Why, Dad?

JUDGE: Because after I got over the disappointment, I started taking out another young lady.

ANDY: And she was Mom?

JUDGE: That's right, Andy.

ANDY: Gee, Dad. I feel better already.

That was Judge Hardy and son on love and marriage. Lew Stone, in reality, was truly Judge Hardy, in a swinging kind of way. Myself? I was in and out of love every two days, never thinking twice, never looking back.

Sometimes the issue was social acceptance.

ANDY: I'm quitting school, Dad. There's a job I can take in South America.

JUDGE: That will upset your mother very much, Andy. She'll miss you.

ANDY: I know, but, Dad, it's time for me to be a man and go out on my own.

JUDGE: Is there any difficulty in school, Andy?

ANDY: It's nothing much.

JUDGE: You know, Andy, I once knew someone who got into difficulty far more serious than what's facing you. He decided that the only thing he could do was travel. He went everywhere. South America, Europe. Everywhere. A long time afterwards, when he came back, he had learned something very important. He hadn't escaped his difficulty at all. He had simply taken it with him. Wherever you travel, no matter how far, you can't escape yourself, son. Now isn't that what you're trying to do? Not escape the others, who aren't getting along with you. Aren't you trying to escape yourself?

ANDY: But I can't go to that prom, Dad. I was supposed to run it and everything's gone wrong and all the kids are sore at me. I just gotta get away.

JUDGE: But from whom, Andy?

ANDY (*thoughtfully*): I guess you're right, Dad. I guess I'm just trying to get away from myself.

That was Andy Hardy, fighting for social acceptance, threatening to leave his home and country. Me? I was a star with friends by the bushel. You couldn't have gotten me away from Hollywood with two dozen bulldozers.

Mr. Stone was a good man and a fine friend. But now that I look back he didn't give me any advice—that I took, that is. Lew was not inclined to interfere with other people's lives. Besides I wasn't asking for advice. If we had talked about major issues, the conversations would have been completely different from what we said before cameras. Take the issue of a car: that would have gone like this:

ME: I'm getting a new car next week.

MR. STONE: What kind?

ME: A Lincoln. I'm going to Detroit. Henry Ford Senior is giving it to me personally.
MR. STONE: Don't strip your gears.

On social acceptance:

ME: I'm throwing a formal party tonight.
MR. STONE: Let me know how many of your friends fall into
the pool.

Lewis Stone lived his life and I lived mine. Mostly, we
were professional associates working together and re-
specting each other's abilities. Some of those man-to-man
talks ran to twenty-five pages of script (so you see, I've
spared you). I could learn them fast and so could Lew,
but once in a while, on camera, one of us would go off on
an ad-lib tangent. Take away the script from some actors
and they're mute. But if I went off script, Lew would pick
me up, ad-libbing just enough to get me on the right
track. If Lew went off script, I could do the same for him.
He was a gifted professional and the real basis of our
association was that professionalism. It was a strong basis.
When Lew died, I lost a part of me that I can't set down.
When people ask if I have any residuals in the Hardy
series, I tell them, truthfully, my residual is having
worked with Lewis Stone.

But professionalism was the extent of it. We were two
actors, not two buddies. I didn't tell him my troubles and
he didn't tell me how to live. Sometimes, in later years,
I've thought that perhaps I should have told Lew things,
that perhaps he could have given me some clues. But hell,

when I was eighteen I didn't have any troubles. I wanted
no clues. I was the hottest young actor in Hollywood.

Movies, like books and plays, attempt to create an
illusion of reality. If they don't create the illusion, they
fail. An audience must believe that the people on the
screen are real people, that their problems on the screen
are real problems, that the tears, which may be glycerine,
are salt and that the leading lady, who actually is in mid-
divorce, is finding eternal happiness in the arms of the
leading man, whom she hardly knows, at the final clinch.

Any time an audience is reminded that the flickerings up
there on the screen are only actors imitating life, the picture fails. Any time an audience thinks, He's only acting,
then an actor isn't acting at all. He is saying lines. It is the
business of the actor to be what he is not and it is the
business of the writer to describe something that never
happens. Strangely, in the double make-believe, we may
find a certain truth.

I mention illusion and reality because I understand why
so many people assumed that I actually was like Andy
Hardy. I understand and I am flattered. For whenever I
convinced an audience that I was Andy Hardy, not
Mickey Rooney, I was doing my job. But that was all.
Andy was typical and naïve and I was atypical.

Lewis Stone was not my confessor, nor were the young
ladies in Andy Hardy's life necessarily the young ladies in
my personal life. As the Hardy series developed, people at
Metro realized they not only had a good thing for themselves and for Lew Stone and for me, they also had a good

thing for starlets. There was, in fact, a standard studio recipe. Take one young actress, pluck her eyebrows, cap her teeth, shape her hairline, pad as required and throw her into the ring with Andy Hardy. Then wait and see. If the public responded, the starlet became a star.

Ann Rutherford was my steady girl in the Hardy movies, but it was a simple matter to add another girl without upsetting the formula of the series. Another girl often worked out as part of the formula. She would appear, I would fall for her, she would fall for someone else and in the end I'd be forgiven by good old reliable Annie.

I remember Lana Turner, whom, of course, I'd known before. She flitted into and out of the Hardy series for a bathing suit scene and some dialogue, on the walk back home, that went about like this:

LANA: Andy?
ME: Yes, Consuella?
LANA: I thought you were taking me home by a shortcut.
ME: I, uh, am.
LANA: But this seems longer than the regular way, Andy.
ME: It is. That's it. It's a short cut that, uh, takes a little longer.
LANA: Andy.
ME: Yes?
LANA: Come hither. (That's a look, not a line.)

We then kissed, a pecking kind of kiss, giggling, as we smacked, like a couple of aging virgins. "That's it," said the director. "Fine." I hurried to my dressing room to finish reading the *Racing Form*, and Lana hurried to a telephone to talk to someone who was ten times as sophis-

ticated as Andy Hardy, and at least five times as sophisticated as Mickey Rooney. That was my real romance with
Lana at the time we were in a picture together. She kissed
me in between phone calls. I kissed her in the middle of a
parlay.

Esther Williams, when she crashed the Hardy series
was a tall, rather gangling swimmer married to a pleasant
fellow who didn't seem to belong to her then and who
doesn't today. They were divorced. That marriage, like so
many of my own, foundered off the Cape of Paradise,
which, as you know, is a suburb of Los Angeles.

I never dated Esther because she was married and
because I didn't like to date girls who could swim rings
around me. It would have been embarrassing in the tank.
Besides, Esther was too *too* tall. (I can see it now, kissing
her good night on the kneecap.)

For the Hardy picture she swam and said some lines.
Her swimming was excellent. Esther was pleasant to work
with and utterly unprofessional. If someone flubbed a line
she went to pieces, even if it wasn't she who flubbed it,
which it usually was. With work, long afterward, she
improved. She had to. It was either that or back to the
tank.

I can't honestly say that Esther Williams acted in a
Hardy picture. She swam in one and from her breast
stroke, big things developed. (Who wants to be tall?)

Kathryn Grayson was very sweet, very lovely and very
talented when she moved into the life of Andy Hardy. She
had a fine voice and she could even act a little. I tried to

date her once or twice but she gave me the impression that she had something going for her higher up in the studio. Maybe she did. But a Hardy picture was what first got the public to pay attention to her high C.

When Donna Reed worked in a Hardy movie, she appeared to be shy and soft-spoken. She was very lady-like, a regular Lady Guinevere.

Donna was ambitious, despite her seeming shyness, and she made a lot of friends. I don't think she made many enemies, although she may have. There was never anything between us. It was with someone else that Donna bit for the bait of marriage. What happened to her first marriage? Like my first, second, third, and fourth, it took the pipe.

Ann Rutherford? A nice girl. A purely professional relationship.

The situation with Judy Garland was different. Once, long ago, my mother asked me why I didn't marry Judy.

"I couldn't do it," I said. "It would be like marrying my sister."

I have always loved Judy without ever being *in* love with her. I think she feels the same way about me. As youngsters, we were too busy being friends to become lovers. Instead, we did the next best, or worst, thing. We became lovers on the screen.

At Ma Lawlor's, during math lessons, Judy and I had swapped mash notes. The notes said such bright and original things as *I love you*, and *I'll always love you*, and *You look beautiful this morning*. Sounds like a bunch of titles for Beatle tunes.

The passion was counterfeit and we both knew it. Only our love of fun was real. The notes were a hell of a lot more amusing than some of the other bright and original things knocking about in Ma Lawlor's classroom. The product of the means is equal to the product of the extremes. Okay, okay. Forget it. *Judy, I love you.* That was more kicks.

I don't know to whom else Judy sent notes. I scattered my pseudo-passion plays carelessly. Theda Roberts and Inez James are two old schoolmates who could convict me of forging love.

Judy, of course, did not need the Hardy series to further her career. She established herself entirely on her own with that classic performance as Dorothy, the little girl who was one part charm and three parts wonder. Or haven't you ever seen *The Wizard of Oz?* Or heard Judy sing Harold Arlen's "Over the Rainbow?" Judy established herself on her own because she had a curious quality. The word is talent.

When Judy came into the Hardy series, performing talent was all she had going for her. She couldn't wiggle like Turner, swim like Williams, purr like Donna Reed or (maybe) hit as high a note as Kathryn Grayson. All Judy could do was entertain. She could make any audience laugh or cry, or, if she were so inclined, get them to stand up and throw silver dollars.

I don't think I knew how good Judy was until I played

opposite her. Her timing was like that of a chronometer. She could deliver a comic line with just the right comic touch, or say a poignant line slowly enough for the poignancy to hit hard but still stay short of schmaltz. She could turn on intensity, as I could turn on intensity, memorize great chunks of script, as I could, ad-lib, as I. Alone, she could take an ordinary scene and by sheer strength of talent make it a scene that people everywhere remembered.

When I was acting with someone like Esther Williams, who was struggling, I played everything straight. Clown, fiddle with timing, ad-lib, and you rattle a novice and ruin a scene. With Judy, it was the other way. We actually tried to rattle each other. Take a scene of tenderness, where the script called for me to whisper something sweet. With a novice, I really would whisper something sweet. With Judy, I might whisper, "Are you wearing a green garter belt today?" Then Judy, when it came time for her to whisper something to me, would hit back the same way.

None of the things we said rival the lines of George Bernard Shaw. We were a couple of teen-age kids, proud of our talent and our poise, trying to make each other lose that poise on camera. I couldn't rattle Judy and she couldn't rattle me. God, we had fun.

The Hardy movies were not my sole means of making a living. In 1939, I made three Hardy pictures, plus *Huckleberry Finn,* and *Babes in Arms,* an exciting musical with Judy. In 1940, I made another Hardy picture, plus *Young*

Tom Edison, and the musical *Strike Up the Band*. In 1941, there were two more Hardy pictures, plus *Men of Boy's Town* and *Babes of Broadway*, a sequel to *Babes in Arms*. The Hardy pictures were the staple, the meat, as the saying goes. They were not the potatoes.

My salary kept soaring. I went to $3,000 a week, then $4,000 and finally to $5,000 a week, which was the highest salary a movie actor could make. In addition, Metro paid me bonuses. My picture schedule was reduced slightly, but not my load of work. Metro kept sending me on personal appearance tours to meet fans. A few times other studios asked Metro to lend me out. When that happened, Metro could ship me out and pocket a large sum. Slavery? Not at $5,000 a week!

During these incredible, wonderful, vanished years, I was still growing up, or trying to. So was Judy. Her life perfectly matched mine. Our friendship grew stronger and stronger.

A few times Judy and I went to Venice, California, or to Ocean Park, or to Santa Monica where we could ride the roller coasters and wander through the fun house. It was something we liked to do together. Wherever either of us went, we were recognized. Somehow it was easier to withstand public pressure when we were together. Most of the people were pleasant, but some of them looked at us as though we were exhibits. Step right this way, ladies and gentlemen, and see the original Andy Hardy and the original girl next door. What's that, madam, can you touch me? Certainly, madam, but they are excitable chil-

dren, you know. Careful, there. Don't feed the entertainers.

It was often a drag to go out. Instead, a lot of times I
took to entertaining at the big house on Densmore. The
guests were usually young actors like myself and most of
the parties were simply extensions of what we did on the
set. I'd play drums or do impersonations. I was always on.
Sidney Miller would play piano. Judy and I would sing
duets: "Manhattan," or "How About You?" Work and fun
were inextricably interwoven. It was impossible to tell
just where one ended and the other began. Our work was
our fun and our fun was our work. Did the Hollywood
kids run around naked, pushing one another into the sack?
No, dammit, we just didn't think of it. We were too busy
being "on."

I drank a little, but not much. None of us drank very
much. None of us smoked reefers, which, looking back,
surprises me. I suppose the positions we held frightened
off even the most ambitious dope pushers. After all, any
man caught selling dope to Andy Hardy would have had
the whole country on his back. A monkey of his own. We
didn't throw bricks through windows, or run orgies, or
pick fights with policemen. We performed. Year after
year, day after day, we performed and performed with all
our hearts.

Once, 1939 I think it was, Judy and I were in New York
playing the Capitol Theater, plugging a picture. The first
show started at 9:15 in the morning and the last show
began at 10:45 at night. We did seven shows a day, and in
between we went to luncheons, dinners, broadcasts,

wakes and bar mitzvahs. (We weren't paid extra for personal appearances; it was all part of the MGM contract. But with bonuses I was earning close to $300,000 a year, so I can't knock the deal.)

The lines outside the Capitol were stretched for blocks. We were stretched, too, stretched pretty thin from the terrific pace we had to maintain. One day at the Capitol, in the middle of a show, Judy collapsed. I heard a commotion in one wing and there was Judy, out flat, a mob of nervous fumblers trying to help her.

All of a sudden I was playing a solo. "Ladies and Gentlemen," I said, "my partner has just been taken ill." I wasn't sure what to do next. We were halfway through a forty-minute show.

"She'll be all right!" somebody shouted from backstage. "Stall 'em, Mickey."

Four score and seven years ago? No. That was out. Someboy else had used it first. Stand on my head? I could do that, but for how long? Whistle "Dixie?" Dullsville. I started a routine about a tennis match and an announcer, the announcer whispering tensely and becoming confused amid the sounds of tennis, such as *zot, plop, plang* (broken string). Then I did a routine about a Joe Louis fight, which included a radio announcer, a ring announcer, crowd noises, and the postfight interview where Joe says it was a good fight and hello, Mother, and, over the body of his victim, Joe thanks everybody who helped make his night so pleasant.

In four or five minutes, Judy was back on stage with me and I realized that if I hadn't mentioned her collapse no one in the audience would have known. That's the sort of trouper Judy was and is. That's one reason why I, like so many others, love the lady.

Often on Sunday mornings I'd drive to the Hollywood house where Judy lived with her mother and her sisters. After breakfast there, and at many times and in many places, we'd talk. I was going to write a musical comedy for her. She was going to sing the songs I wrote. We'd do our won play. We'd capture Broadway. We'd be the most successful team in history. During those distant, well-remembered days, we launched many ships at many ports. Later on, when Judy and I grew older, we found out that most of the ships had sailed away without us.

These were the halcyon years, and heedless. I suppose, deep underneath, I knew that it couldn't last forever. I wouldn't be No. 1 at the box office or the world forever. I might not even make $5,000 a week forever. I supposed I knew, but it was hidden away. I didn't want to see it.

How could I know about failure? I'd never failed at anything. How could I know about solitude? I was always in a crowd and the crowd was always urging, "Entertain, Mick, baby. Do your stuff, baby." How could I know about myself? I spent all my time being someone else.

I wasn't reliable. I'd make a date with a girl, get interested in another one and not show up. Then, two days later, I'd break a date with the second girl. I didn't send Christmas cards or Christmas gifts. I meant to, as I meant to keep my dates, but so much was going on that I could never get my life organized. It didn't seem to matter, then.

Disorganized is good enough, isn't it, buddy? You stay organized and look for work. I'll stay disorganized and be the top star.

I wasn't old enough to drink legally and I didn't much care for liquor, but I had to show whom—myself?—that I could drink. At some parties in Dave Chasen's restaurant, I'd tell Sig Frohlich, "Hey, meet me in the can and bring along a straight shot." Big deal. Big, brash deal.

When we had a short day on the set, I'd grab Sig. "Come on. We can still make the fourth race." Sig, who was older, could buy the mutuel tickets. Underage, I bet on the races. Big deal. Big, brash deal.

I dated dozens of different girls and I flirted with hundreds to show whom—myself?—that I could flirt. But it was almost always trivial, invariably brief and immature. The big movie star can date a lot of girls. Big deal. Big, brash deal. (But lots of them didn't date me for me—not the real me—they dated The Entertainer.)

I mixed thoughtful seconds with thoughtless weeks, warmth with bursts of fury, false humility with real pride. Sig and I were talking about it recently. "You mixed good and bad," Sig said, "like a cow that gives a bucket of grade A milk and then kicks over the bucket."

What could my mother have done to warn me, even if she had known that warnings were in order? Not very much, I'm afraid. In most family relationships, the child lives off the generosity of his parents. They pay his bills and, in a showdown, one parent can always clinch the pennant by saying, "No allowance for the next two weeks."

In our big place at Densmore, the situation might have worked in reverse. I was supporting the household. I didn't use it consciously, but I always knew I could use it if I had to. Actually, a lot of the money went into trust funds for my mother and for myself, but the living expenses, the high-living expenses, came out of my movie income. It's hard to discipline, to counsel any headstrong teen-ager. It is impossible to discipline a headstrong teen-ager who is independently wealthy. *I Was a Teen-Age Breadwinner.* A movie title, or maybe something for TV. We might be able to get a baking company to sponsor it.

The studio, of course, was interested in counseling me. In fact, they had a man named Les Peterson, who was vice-president in charge of Mickey Rooney. But in truth, Peterson was not in charge of me; he was in charge of my image. The primary concern of Louis B. Mayer, Les Peterson and everyone else at Metro was to keep the image of Mickey Rooney clean, shining and as close to the image of Andy Hardy as possible. A personification of perfection is what they wanted me to be. For a time, Peterson was a confidant and friend. "Don't do this, don't do that," preserving the image and robbing me of fun, or a sneak drink, or a ticket on a winner or a loser. It didn't strike me for a while that Les Peterson was not my friend at all. He was a friend of Metro-Goldwyn-Mayer, Incorporated.

Les is gone from show business now. He's an executive at a bank. Perhaps there his conservatism may be appreciated. Personally, I believe his constant surveillance and interference had much to do with my youthful emotional rebellion.

Some people have written of Louis B. Mayer as though he were an ogre. They may have their reasons; I have none. In later years I fought with Mayer and we each got ugly with the other. Mayer had his impossible moments, but he was, after all, the man who kept the store going. I respect his memory as someone who could do a job in show business, and show business is my business.

But what advice could Mayer give me? What advice could I ask of him? I didn't trot off to see the studio head with minor personal matters. Nor does a studio head concern himself with the psyche of his actors, unless the actors are about to break up themselves or the studio. The boss wants to keep the actors working happily and I was doing just that. Mr. Mayer and I were friends in those days. It was on a very shallow level, but we were friends.

He liked me and the money I was making for Metro, and on my twentieth birthday he gave me a pregnant horse. Away from the studio Mr. Mayer, who had started out in real poverty, was a dedicated horse breeder. He owned a lot of horses, some of the greatest in the world. My interest in horses and bookmakers was no secret. So when I was twenty, Mayer gave me a mare named Stereopticon, who was about to foal. Potentially, it was an immensely valuable gift. If the foal grew swift as Whirlaway, it could be worth hundreds of thousands of dollars. I was grateful and delighted and convinced that the foal would indeed be fast as Whirlaway. Or faster.

I shipped Stereopticon out to a ranch and every week-end, I'd drive out to watch her belly swell. I was an expectant godfather to a horse and I relished the role.

One night in March, the call came. Stereopticon was about to deliver herself a Whirlaway. It was late, but I dressed and headed for the ranch.

Fred Pankey, by then my stepfather for some 12 years, got on a phone in private almost as soon as I hung up. He started calling animal men, asking if they had a zebra in stock. Hollywood, of course, is a center of the animal business. Build a prop jungle, stock it with tame tigers and you've saved the cost of sending a crew to India. Fred must have called half a dozen Hollywood animal men. His scheme was simple: He intended to slip a zebra into Stereopticon's stall. Then when I arrived, looking for the young Whirlaway, I'd see the zebra. The vet was to say, "A medical phenomenon, Mickey. I've never heard of anything like it."

"A zebra must have gotten in first," Fred was going to say.

Then everyone would look at my face.

They underestimated my love for horses. Frantic to see the colt, I drove to the ranch à la Barney Oldfield and I beat the zebra to the stall. Instead of a striped refugee from Africa, I saw a leggy little colt, Stereopticon's real offspring. The mare had foaled as fast as I had driven. I'm sorry about the zebra joke, as I look back on it. The zebra might have run faster than the colt did.

Because of Fred's spoiled joke, we decided to call the colt In-In-Time. He was a nice colt, friendly—so friendly he never wanted to leave the other horses. He liked their company. We gave him the best of care, the best of training and, a few years later when he was ready to go, I hired Johnny Longden to ride him. Longden still is one of the finest jockeys in the world.

When In-In-Time first ran at Santa Anita, Longden got him out of the gate in a hurry and the colt ran off and hid from the field. At the far turn, In-In-Time was seven lengths in front. Count 'em. One, two, three, four, five, six, seven lengths. That's my colt. I turned around and smiled. "I told you we have a hell of a horse, Fred," I said. Then I turned back. In-In-Time was twelfth. He'd stopped as if he'd been shot by an arrow. That was how In-In-Time ran that day and that was how he always ran. All promise. No cash.

I sold In-In-Time after a while and I lost track of him. If he isn't dead now, I know where he is. In the homestretch on some county fairground track, thirty-seven lengths behind the field.

My interest in gambling then, like my interest in gambling now, was not motivated by money. I didn't want to get rich gambling. I already had become rich acting. I liked to win bets for the pleasure of victory. I liked the sensation of tension becoming stronger and stronger, the sensation that culminates in a few furious instants of triumphant action. You have that when you entertain, and when your longshot outruns the field.

I brought my father, Joe Yule, Sr., to Hollywood during these gaudy years. We got to be friends, but my father could give me no advice, no words of caution. It had been so long. What he saw in me, I suppose, was part flesh of his flesh and part someone who had done what he'd always wanted to do—make it big in show business. My father and I didn't have the standard father-son relationship. I was happy enough that we could at least become friends.

So much was grinding within me. Too much. I had money, dates, friends, more invitations than I could accept, more adulation than was good for me. Still, something was grinding. My size, again. Was it my size? Was it the fact that for all my rewards, I still stood only five-feet three-inches? Was it the fact that because I stood small some people expected me to be small? Not "Act your age," but, "Act your size." Did that cut me?

Someone once asked Eddie Arcaro, when Eddie was still facing death every afternoon, why he didn't quit riding. Arcaro didn't need the money. "Because," the greatest of all jockeys said, "if I quit riding, I'd be just another little man."

That was Eddie's problem. I don't think it was mine. Sig Frohlich has told me that the way I was, always entertaining, always filling a room with sound, made everyone forget within a few moments that I was short. Certainly, I gave size little thought. Size wasn't what kept things grinding in my guts.

I had done plenty. I had to do more. If I proved myself in twelve different ways, I'd have to prove myself in a thirteenth. I must have inherited in some gene a drive that pushed me harder and harder. The more successful I was, the more successful I had to become. I'd acted, sung, danced, drunk, gambled. I'd met President Roosevelt and Henry Ford. My face was postered all over America. What was there left for me at twenty? What was there left for me to do? Try marriage. That was where this drive pushed me next. My drive and the beauty of Ava Gardner.

II

I saw Ava Gardner one afternoon on a set at Metro when we were shooting *Babes on Broadway.* The year was 1940. Ava was dressed like a princess. I was dressed like a girl.

Don't get me wrong. I was doing an impersonation of Carmen Miranda, the late dancer from Brazil, who was wild, extroverted and who enjoyed a rage in the early 1940's. I was wearing a long, colorful skirt, a bodice blouse and a hat upon which grew a fruit garden. (I did look good, if I say so myself.)

Metro had just signed Ava and a publicity man was showing her around the lot. When she appeared, everything in me stopped. My heart. My breathing. My thinking. I was conservative in those days, it was all of five seconds before I told myself I had seen the girl I was going to marry.

I walked over in my samba skirt, my wedge shoes, my bodice blouse, my fruity hat. "Hello," I said. "I'm Mickey Rooney."

"This is Miss Ava Gardner," the publicity man said.

"Hello," said Miss Ava Gardner.

She drawled it a little. She was fresh from Wilson, North Carolina. Like a thousand other pretty girls, she had come west to crash Hollywood, after winning some kind of beauty contest back home. Metro had signed her to a no-risk contract. They were paying Ava $75 a week. In exchange, she was to pose for still photographs and to work with a diction specialist in order to erase the drawl. If Ava failed to make it—and most would-be movie stars do fail—Metro wouldn't be out much. Just a few dozen $75 checks.

I say pretty girls. Ava was unlike the thousand other pretty girls because she was so much more than pretty. How did she look? Black hair, animal litheness, a face that bespoke both reserve and passion. How did Miss Ava Gardner look? Sleek and proud and graceful and tender and infinitely infinitely feminine. Miss Ava Gardner looked like and was love.

"Would you care to dine with me tonight?"

"No," Ava said. "I'm busy tonight, Mr. Rooney."

It took five nights to break down the wall. A lot of girls were easy to date in those days. They wanted to date me because I was a famous movie star and if they played me exactly right, some of the fame and maybe some of the magic might rub off on them. Then there were a few girls who liked me for my brash and arrogant self. I can't think of any offhand, but there must have been at least one. There had to be.

My technique in those days was a combination of early Neanderthal and late Freud. I'd approach for a bombing run confidently, confessing that yes, it was true, I was the

one, the only, the original Mickey Rooney. Of course the
girl already knew who I was, my face being famous and
hanging out. But now I gave her a chance to hear my
romantic voice. Once I had decided to give the trembling
lady a break and let her meet the man who wasn't Andy
Hardy, I could have waited for a reaction to develop.
Could have, but didn't. I'd go from the introduction into a
monologue and then, amid candlelight and violins, I'd
rasp out a few impersonations. As I say, I was always
"on." I was no counterpuncher. I always had to get my
blows in first.

Sometimes I feel that what I really wanted from those
half-forgotten ladies was the same thing I wanted from an
audience: applause. Once the girls liked my act, I'd
gotten what I wanted most. I'm not saying I didn't hop
into and out of as many beds as would accept me. But
these little affairs were always transient, always brief. I'd
made my conquest before we hit the sack when the girl
had said, after one of my routines, "Gee, Mickey, you're
wonderful." The sack was the dessert course or the apéri-
tif. Thanks. It was very nice. I'll call you in the morning.
And by the way, did you really like my impersonations,
dear, uh, uh? I'm sorry. I can't seem to remember your
name.

What results from an approach like this is a series of
essentially meaningless affairs. I know it is fashionable to
assert that sex, without love, is empty. It is fashionable
and absurd. Sex for the sake of sex can be just fine. When
I say meaningless, I imply that within the scheme of my
forty-four years on this planet, these affairs have little

significance. They were not meaningless in the immediacy of their happenings. Some of the most pleasant nights of my late boyhood were spent with ladies I did not know.

I think this is a stage every normal human being undergoes, man and woman, provided he or she is honest. We are all lonely, all curious, all afraid of the future, of our emotions. Somebody, F. Scott Fitzgerald perhaps, has pointed out that it is always three o'clock in the morning in the darkness of our souls. And so it was. And so it is. And so it will be. Against this, we seek to illuminate that blackness, to batter down the battlements of loneliness, to purge our beings of their terrors. How better than in the fusion of two humans into one? How better than in this deathlike tableau, which, for all its pangs and writhings and groanings, is the very negation of what it most resembles, the ultimate dread, that other bed where other pangs and writhings and groanings end with death.

When I found a lady who both liked my impersonations and was willing to accept me, I was elated. But because I was young, the instant elation quickly turned to instant boredom. I'd move on to someone else, as quickly as possible. The reason I never became deeply involved with anyone before Ava was simply that I did not give myself the chance. I admired a face and a body. I made the face brighten. I took the body. I left before bothering to learn if, besides the face and the body, the lady was also a person, even as I.

This is not unique, nor do I think it is abnormal. Men lust, and so do women. Some seem to settle down in later years, their fires banked, but as long as man is not senile and possesses courage, he accepts his own lusts. I admire more the man who has the courage to pursue the lady who arouses him than the man who tries to deny that he is aroused, then goes home and throws bricks at his wife. Isn't there a happy medium? There well may be. There is no surplus of happy mediums. Human beings, for all their high deeds, are vastly, infinitely, privately troubled about the meanings and uses of sex.

Had Ava Gardner done a handstand on meeting me, our romance might have ended on the spot. Had she come at me, as some other women, obviously determined to capitalize on my fame, it would have died in some other spot a few weeks later. But no, Ava didn't seem to give a damn who I was, or what I was, or what I could do for her, or how much money I was making. Although she wanted to become an actress, she seemed to be disinterested in the box office king of the world.

The first time she condescended to go out with me, I drove—a red convertible by this time—to her apartment on Franklin Avenue in Hollywood. It wasn't much of a neighborhood and it wasn't much of an apartment. Ava lived there with her sister Beatrice. I bought us dinner at Chasen's. Then I took her dancing somewhere.

"Would you like to hear me impersonate Cary Grant?" I said at one point.

"Would you like to impersonate Cary Grant?" Ava said.

"Sure," I said. "I do it great."

"Well, go ahead, if you want to," Ava said.

I impersonated Cary.

"I also do Jimmy Cagney," I said.

"That's interesting," Ava said, looking around the room.

I impersonated Jimmy.

"How about Lionel Barrymore playing Dr. Gillespie?" I said.

"How about him?" Ava said.

I impersonated Lionel very well!

Nothing was happening.

Here was a beautiful girl, ambitious enough to come to Hollywood, who didn't seem to give a damn that I was Mickey Rooney, or that I had talent, or that I had influence at the studio. She'd been eating in hash houses, but she took Chasen's, where the hash is made from prime ribs, completely in stride. This girl, whom I wanted, didn't seem to want me. Me. Mickey Rooney. Well, by God, she was going to want me. I'd show her. I'd get her. The hook was baited.

That night, as we were standing in the hallway of the second-rate building where she lived, I said, "Ava, will you marry me?"

Her eyes narrowed slightly. "You must be crazy," she said. Then, more cheerfully, she added, "Good night."

I climbed into my convertible and drove off into the evening. And the night seemed deeper now and more mysterious. There was a new world to conquer, a world in the shape of a woman who was more compelling, more magnificent than I could even begin to suspect.

Now it was finished. Now it was done.

The brash, arrogant boyhood had run its course. The

seeds, which seemed to sparkle in my hands, had all been sown. Now it was done.

The burlesque halls. Mickey McGuire. Puck. Andy Hardy. The house on Densmore. Each was a triumph. There had been only triumphs, no defeats.

Hiya, Mick. Say, aren't you Mickey Rooney? Sign this, Mick. Here's your new contract, Mick. Mr. Rooney, I've *so* wanted to meet you.

Hello, there, ladies and gentlemen. For my first routine I'd like to do an autobiographical number called *The Boy Who Couldn't Fail.*

Hey, Sig, sneak me a shot of booze. Hey, agents, run me an errand. Hey, directors, you got the scene all wrong. I oughta play it this way. Oh, yeah? Well, who the hell's the star of this show?

Forgive me my boyhood. Forgive me, victims of my thoughtlessness. Forgive me, friends whom I offended, ladies I misused, innocents I assaulted with loudness. Forgive me, forgive me.

Somewhere beyond, the Fates were unforgiving. Slowly, excruciatingly, they started to turn my world around, turn it against me. I didn't know. I didn't care. But now it was done.

5 * *Not Wisely,*
But Too Well

I

Will the meeting please come to order? Thank you,
gentlemen. Our subjects today are the wives of Mickey
Rooney. A question? Yes. How can you tell the wives
apart? By the numbers, sir, by the numbers.

Now we're going to go over this once, briefly, and then
maybe we can take it up in a little more detail.

To begin with we have Mrs. Ava Gardner Rooney,
brunette and lovely. Later Mrs. Ava Gardner Shaw. Still
later Mrs. Ava Gardner Sinatra. Now again Miss Ava
Gardner. Ava was Mrs. Rooney for less than two years. In
Los Angeles divorce case D–237,213, her charge was
"grievous mental suffering." Ava Gardner Rooney. Number One.

Next we see Mrs. Betty Jane Rase Rooney. Also bru-
nette and lovely. Formerly Miss Birmingham, Alabama.
Later Mrs. Betty Jane Rase Baker. Still later Mrs. Betty
Jane Kessel. Betty Jane was Mrs. Rooney for four years.

She became the mother of Mickey Rooney, Junior, and Timothy Rooney. In Los Angeles divorce case D–360,690, her charge was "mental cruelty." Betty Jane Rase Rooney. Number Two.

Next we find Mrs. Martha Vickers Rooney, auburn-haired and lovely. Formerly Mrs. Martha Vickers Lyles. Later Mrs. Martha Vickers Rojas. Martha was Mrs. Rooney for two years. Mother of Teddy Rooney. In Los Angeles divorce case D–416,884, her charge was "extreme cruelty." Martha Vickers Rooney. Number Three.

And in this corner we have Mrs. Elaine Mahnken Rooney, red-haired and lovely. Elaine was Mrs. Rooney for almost seven years, a track record. In Santa Monica divorce case S.D.M. 18,328, her charge was "cruelty." Mrs. Elaine Mahnken Rooney. Number Four.

These records can be inspected at Room 112, County Court House, Los Angeles, California.

Are you clear, then, on all the numbers? Good. What's that? You're clear on something else? What else are you clear on? Oh, you say *Mister* Mickey Rooney must be a pretty cruel son of a bitch?

I'd be a little careful there. You're oversimplifying.

It seems like a joke, I suppose. Four divorces and five wives. All men are polygamous, but marrying five times is something for a third-rate comic opera. Except, of course, it isn't comic at all. I lived with all these lovely women. I loved them, or at the least I told myself I did. I fought with them, made up with them, drank with them, slept

with them and finally, in scenes of terrible intensity, broke
with them (or they with me).

No, four divorces isn't funny. It's no funnier than making fifty alimony payments. It's no funnier than finding
your wife in love with someone new; no funnier than
sitting in a lawyer's office and, amid the thick books and
the stacked briefs, letting your life be opened like a
wound. It is no funnier than looking at a child, your child,
and knowing that forever after this boy and you are condemned to a life apart. Oh, yes, you know it isn't funny
but you also know that no one can build a monument of
tears. So on television you grin and make small jokes
about alimony.

"And if I laugh at any mortal thing, 'tis that I may not
weep." Lord Byron, a man acquainted with divorce.

The thing is that looking backward, I can see why I
married each woman when I did. In fact, I see a certain
inevitability. I *had* to marry each woman when I did.
That doesn't make it very much easier. Understanding
mistakes is better than self-hatred. Better still, is not to
make the mistakes at all.

But there are children born of the marriages, born of
love, children who have a right to exist. Do *I*, then, have a
right to call these marriages mistakes?

"Mr. Rooney, how short are you?"

"Since my last divorce, roughly $300,000."

And if I laugh at any mortal thing.

In 1965, I celebrated my twenty-fourth wedding anniversary. Five wives, but still twenty-four years. Con-

gratulations, Ava. Congratulations, B.J. Congratulations, Mart. Congratulations, Red. Congratulations, Barb.

Laughter (but only from the audience).

I am going to put aside my professional career, my soldiering and my long decline now, and mention only what is significant to the issues at hand, the Mrs. Mickey Rooneys. It would be too confusing for me to use a camera with a super-wide lens. Five marriages and four divorces are sufficiently confusing unto themselves. Besides, in my life, as in this book, they represent a single, specialized chapter.

Where was I? Oh, yes. I believe I was driving off into a warm California night, away from the second-rate apartment of Miss Ava Gardner, bored beauty.

Back home, in the big house on Densmore, I considered the situation. Faced with a lady who was immune to my charms and to my fame, I decided there was only one solution. I'd overexpose her to each. I would be more charming than I ever had been. I would run Miss Ava Gardner a chase through Hollywood, my Hollywood, to bedazzle those dark Carolinian eyes.

I called early the next day.

"I enjoyed last night very much, Ava."

She was sleepy, and sleepily she thanked me.

"You don't have a car, do you?" I said.

"You know I don't. I can't afford a car."

"Well, it sure must be a drag for you to get to the studio every morning."

"Oh, it's not too bad," Ava said.

"Suppose I stop by and pick you up. You know. Drive you to work."

"All right," Ava said, with small enthusiasm.

Picking up Ava became part of my morning routine. My evening routine was not much different. Most nights it began at Ava's apartment.

Perhaps a more mature man, confronted with a potentially passionate but currently dispassionate Miss Gardner, would have played on her with winning subtlety. Perhaps, but I doubt it. Ava does strange things to men. Artie Shaw, wordly and literate, and Frank Sinatra, worldly and assertive, played on her no better than I when, long years afterward, their time for Ava came round.

My own youthful response to Ava's aloofness was to employ what they call in basketball the all-court press. I invaded every aspect of her life. I was always available for such services as chauffeuring, dinner purchasing, dancing, squiring, impersonating and proposing. Ava in turn was unavailable. She gave me neither her heart, nor her body.

When it became apparent that my dating Ava was more than just another trivial affair, red flags were hoisted at MGM. To the studio, it was a question of the image again. "I don't know why you keep bothering with that girl," Les Peterson told me. "Sure she's pretty, but take it from me, a guy as successful as you should be playing the field." I can only assume that Peterson, pretending to offer advice, was actually executing orders issued in the throne room of Louis B. Mayer. Andy Hardy married? We can't have that. What about all the little girls who want Andy for themselves? Will they stop going to the movies? Listen, Les, we got to keep that little bastard from getting married. Talk to him like a friend, Les. You know how to do it. For the studio, Les. (And for the image.)

My mother, my stepfather and my father were not wildly enthusiastic about Ava. For all my fame, I was not yet twenty-one. What does a twenty-year-old know of marriage? they reasoned, as though there were any reasoning with me.

So there it was. The studio didn't want me to marry Ava. My family was unenthusiastic. Ava was unenthusiastic. The wheels ground more quickly. I had to have her.

It's been suggested that Ava finally broke down because she saw in me not only a husband but a stepping-stone. I think the error here is a confusion between Ava as she is now, hard-living, hard-driving, and Ava as she was then, rather naïve and unpossessed of fierce ambition. (I lived with the lady. I know.) At an early age, Ava must have discovered that her appearance gave her remarkable powers over men. But as I was young at twenty, Ava was young at eighteen. We were a couple of kids, not a couple of conspirators.

Pursuit, by red convertible, continued. We went to premieres where I was recognized and where bystanders cheered when I appeared, then asked in loud whispers,

"Who's the girl?" We went dancing at the Palladium.
Every few moments somebody stopped me, or called my
name, or stared. We went to Chasen's again and again,
and I introduced her to the great stars of the day. I called
for Ava, escorted her, spun her into my wild and hectic
orbit. She took it calmly, as though she had been born into
my world. This frantic exciting arena must have seemed
strange to her, but she adamantly refused to be awed.

In one respect, my courtship of Ava would have delighted virtue-loving Louis B. Mayer. It was an Andy
Hardy kind of courtship. She gave me her lips for a good-
night kiss. She gave me soft hands to hold. She gave me
nothing more.

You see, Ava as she is now, buffeted by three broken
marriages and Lord knows how many other tragedies,
makes her peace with existence as best she can. What the
marriage to Shaw and the marriage to Sinatra took out of
her, I do not know. But I do know that life has made Ava
Gardner unhappy in many ways, as it has made me
unhappy in many ways. Some call Ava wild. That's Ava
now. But when I speak of her as a naïve girl from Carolina, who made a good-night kiss the end of sex, I am not
simply romanticizing my first love. I am describing Ava
then—Ava as she lived and breathed and thought before
life had inflicted very many scars. I am not now what I
was in 1940. Nor are you. Nor is Ava.

I don't know how I finally won the lady. Perhaps she
was tired of spurning me and gave way to fatigue. Perhaps she loved me. I'd like to think so and besides I know
this: Ava, like myself, did not intend to get married so

that she could later experience the embarrassment of divorce.

From that first night, almost every time I dated Ave, I closed the proceedings with a proposal. I don't know exactly how many times I proposed. I stopped counting after twenty-five. I asked in as many ways as I knew:

Will you marry me?

Will *you* marry me?

Will you *marry* me?

Will you marry *me*?

For a while, she was content to dismiss the proposals as idiocy. "Marry you, Mickey? I hardly know you. Please don't start that again." Then gradually her counters became less sure. "Marriage is a serious thing, Mickey. Maybe the most important thing in the world to a girl. I don't want to marry anyone until I'm positive it will work out." Finally there came hints that she was beginning to take me seriously.

"What would our life be like, Mickey?"

"Well, you'd act and I'd act and we'd both be big stars and we'd have a ball."

"I mean our life together, Mickey, at home."

"We'd have a ball."

Sometimes my intensity exploded and I promised her mansions, minks and cars. "Anything, Ava, anything." If she had asked me to promise to wash dishes every night, I would have done it. If she had asked me to buy her a studio, I would have tried. I had to have her and the only way I knew was to offer every particle of myself.

The more I wanted Ava, the more Metro pressed me to

stay away, and the more Metro pressed, the surer I was that I must possess her. Ultimately, the night of acceptance came, but even then I did not possess her entirely. It was kiss and talk, no more.

"All right, Mickey," Miss Ava Gardner said, slowly. "I'll marry you."

We kissed for a long time. Then I said, "When?"

"Well, you'll have to work that out with the studio, won't you? You'll have to see when there's time in your shooting schedule."

"The hell with the schedule," I said. "We'll get married tomorrow." We didn't. I had to work it out with the studio, and the studio wouldn't agree that my shooting schedule could go to hell.

Once I was engaged to Ava, Metro capitulated as gracefully as it could. The bigwigs insisted on a small wedding, hidden away from fans and reporters, but that was their only soreheaded demand. A few days before I was to marry Ava, Louis Mayer threw me a bachelor party in a huge studio dining room. His whole roster of male stars paraded in.

Lew Stone arrived, had a cocktail. He didn't try to give me a fatherly talk. Clark Gable was there, and Spencer Tracy and Robert Taylor. The luncheon, which was supposed to be a roasting, turned out to be a barbecue. I spun on the spit.

Someone suggested words that a husband can utter on coming home at 3:15 A.M. "Lipstick, nothing. Those are red pencil marks. I've been down at the office all night and, honey, is the business taking a beating!"

Someone else gave me sex counsel. "Take it easy, until your muscles adjust. A sprained back is hard to explain to the columnists."

There was advice on infighting ("watch her knees"), suggestions on technique ("nibble her ear, but not too much. It ain't like it was a steak sandwich, kid") and, naturally, gifts. Many, many gifts from many wonderful people. Some of them, the people, are gone, but I remember them—you do too.

Oh, I still hear the voices, see the scene! Hey, Mickey, you're finally taking the plunge. Hey, Mickey, have another drink. Hey, Mickey, that's a hell of a beautiful girl you got there. Be careful. The sounds, eternal sounds of ribaldry. The sounds of laughter. Glasses raised. A company of men saluting me.

"Thanks, fellows, I appreciate all your jokes, you horny bastards, and the first guy I see looking hard at Mrs. Rooney gets a right hand to the teeth."

Cheers.

More voices. Hey, Mickey, you know about the pebbles in the sink. You know that in the first year of marriage, every time you love your wife you put a pebble in the sink. After that, whenever you love your wife, you take a pebble out of the sink. Hey, Mickey. You know what? You'll never empty the sink.

Ribaldry, laughter, the faces of Gable, Taylor, Tracy, the story about the first year and pebbles in the sink. If someone had told me that after the first year of marriage,

I wouldn't be sharing my sink—much less my life—with Ava Gardner Rooney, I'd have thrown that threatened right hand, then and there.

We were married at a nondenominational church in the town of Ballard, California, on January 10, 1941. Ava was nineteen. I was twenty-one, legally a man.

Ballard is a town lying inland, north of Los Angeles and south of San Francisco. It was selected by Les Peterson as the ideal location for marriage in obscurity. "You don't want one of those big Hollywood weddings," Peterson told me. "With all the fans and the reporters and photographers, it would be a circus."

"We don't want one of those big Hollywood weddings," I told Ava. "With all the fans and the reporters and photographers, it would be a circus."

"I don't know, Mickey," Ava said. "A big wedding might be nice."

"Nah, we'll do it quietly," I said. "That's the way it ought to be."

"Well, if you think so."

"Sure, I think so, honey. Don't worry. I know what I'm doing."

Me know what I was doing? That was the misstatement of my twenty-one years. But Ava must have thought I did. I was a big little man in Hollywood. I seemed to know my way around.

The studio's thinking was this: If we can't stop the son of a bitch from getting married, at least we can make him get married out of sight. Tell him, Les. Hush it up, Les. Be his buddy, Les. You tell him.

There were two cars and seven bodies in the wedding party: my mother, my father, my stepfather, Les Peterson, Beatrice Gardner and, oddly enough, Ava and myself. We started for Ballard early in the morning and arrived at about eleven o'clock. The service was brief. I don't remember being nervous. Ava was radiant as I quickly slipped on a ring marked *Love Forever*. At least that was what we saw. We didn't know that the ring was really marked (with invisible ink) only *Number One*.

Afterwards, I walked over to Les Peterson. "We've been together a hell of a lot," I said, "and now I think we've come to a parting of the ways."

"I guess so," Peterson said, a little nervously. (Would the studio approve his leaving me alone for my wedding night?)

"See ya, Les," I said, loudly.

"See ya, Mick."

The extras in our small, brief wedding scene piled into one car and headed toward Los Angeles. Ava and I slipped into the other car and headed toward Monterey where we had reserved a little place close by the sea.

I drove quickly and suddenly we were there and day was gone and it was night in Monterey, with the sounds of the surf and the sight of the moon and we were two young people in love, and I walked into a bathroom to put on my pajamas.

I hadn't been nervous, but now my nerves spun me like a tornado. The reaction had begun. I was married. That magnificent brunette, sliding into a nightgown just a door away, was my wife. For all my life I'd have the lady to myself. Would she tire of me? Or I of her? Ten thousand breakfasts together. The hell with that. Ten thousand nights. Ava Gardner Rooney. My wife. It all caught up with me. Panic.

I had been putting on pajamas for most of my twenty-one years. Now, with Ava in waiting beyond the door, I forgot how. My hands were shaking when I reached for my pajama tops and started to step into them. The pajama arms were too short for my legs. I reached for the bottoms and pulled them over my head. I was temporarily blinded. Ava was waiting. I had to get to her, had to be with her. I knew about entering a scene. I wasn't going to walk into this one stark naked. I had to put on the damn pajamas. Putting on my pajamas on my first wedding night took me all of twenty minutes.

Ava was waiting, lying very still in her gown. Then again there was the sound of the surf and the faint glow of moonlight and we were two young people together now, together at last. We were man and woman, Ava and I, alone and young and loving. I was impatient, so probably inept.

But not to Ava. There was no way in which she could have measured my ineptitude. For I was the first man ever to possess all of Ava Gardner. I was proud.

We spent four days in Monterey. Or I spent four days there. Ava endured them.

What does an impassioned young groom carry with him

on his honeymoon? This impassioned young groom carried golf clubs. Togetherness, you see. The husband golfs and the wife caddies.

"Good morning, darling," Ava said, awakening to find herself a bride.

"Hiya, honey!"

"Oh, I feel so lazy. Let's just laze around all day."

"Nah. Come on, honey. There's a helluva golf course here I want to play."

"Golf!!"

"You'll love the course. It's beautiful."

"I don't play golf. Do we have to go?"

"Wait till you see the course, honey," I said.

We went and Ava walked along, her graceful leggy walk. I hacked away. No. Hacked isn't the right word. I'd gotten my game down into the seventies. I was playing well. If my honeymoon had been as successful as my short approach game, it would have been a creditable score.

There's a clue to my character here that may give psychiatrists and golf pros some delight. For a wedding trip with Ava Gardner, I brought along matched woods and irons. Still playing Puck—what a fool this mortal be.

We were both in shock in Monterey. Married. Hooked. If you ever were a kid on a honeymoon, you know the feeling. Doomed. A house. A family. Married. Help! But even through the shock, the disruptive pattern that was to tear our particular marriage apart began immediately to assert itself.

I loved Ava very much. To show my love, I hit seven-irons. "See," I wanted to say. "See what I can do. Look how well I hit golf shots. Aren't you proud of me, Ava, hitting such beautiful golf shots just for you?" That was what I wanted to say and perhaps should have said. But that wasn't how I talked to my lady. "Think I can reach the green from here with a five?" That was what I did say. I kept my head down and stroked nicely, concentrating on the golf, and Ava walked her graceful leggy walk.

I was playing as well as I could because I wanted to show Ava how good I was. At golf. At everything else. I loved Ave. But to her eyes, and to the eyes of anyone else, it must have seemed that I loved only myself. This lack of consideration has been the constant prelude to dissolved marriages, only hell, I didn't mean it. I didn't intend to be inconsiderate, I just didn't recognize what I was.

I had no real idea of what marriage was, what marriage meant. Some youngsters seem to sense these things by instinct. Others ask advice and accept at least a part of what they're told. I sensed nothing and hadn't been listening to anybody, except once in a while to Les Peterson. And there was little wisdom to be acquired there, since he merely followed the orders given to him.

My first dim view of marriage was that it had to be a test of masculine strength. I'm not referring to bed. I mean I thought that marriage was a small dictatorship in which the husband is the dictator and the wife is the underling. What should a husband do? Precisely what he wants to do. What should a wife do? Precisely what the husband wants, also. In those few days at Monterey I called the shots in eating, drinking, sleeping, golfing and lovemaking. What an impossible son of a bitch I must have been.

To this day, I don't think Ava has forgiven me for my selfishness, my stupidity and my clumsiness in those beginning moments of marriage. I sometimes wonder if I've forgiven myself.

The disaster of the honeymoon foreshadowed the disaster of our relationship. Wherever we were, whatever we did, this beautiful, complicated lady and I, I was the one who always assumed center stage.

Ava is a lady of strong passions, something which has mixed merit, one of her passions being rage. Maybe you've read newspaper stories of tantrums Ava has thrown at the press and others. I don't know if the stories are true, but I've read them myself. They are believable.

On our honeymoon, her rage, if it existed at all, was buried deep. Her passions then were all channeled in a single direction. But the quality of rage has always been part of Ava. We set up house in Hollywood, a selfish young man and an angry young woman. From the beginning we had a lot going against us.

I rented a small comfortable home in Stone Canyon. There wasn't much land around it. There weren't even sterling silver fixtures in the bathrooms. Why hadn't I taken over the big house on Densmore? Well, starting a fresh life in fresh surroundings seemed like a good idea to both of us. Besides, my family was used to the big house; I wasn't anxious to disrupt them. Finally, we expected a good deal of pressure from the press and from the public. Somehow a large house by its very size seems to symbolize pressure. This one point we'd talked through thoroughly before getting married. A small modest house seemed best. Perhaps we were wrong. Certainly I had money enough to buy a showplace. Our marriage itself was on display. Maybe it belonged in a vast, expensive showplace. At any rate, no matter where we lived, it couldn't have worked out worse than it did in the comfortable little house in Stone Canyon.

From there we resumed our careers, which between us totaled a career and a half. Mine was soaring. Ava's had barely begun. Each day I went off to the studio to act. Some days Ava went there, too, but only to pose for publicity pictures. My career, my life, were overflowing. But Ava had little to occupy her time, aside from me.

In the beginning, Ava was completely intent on becoming a wife and homemaker. She cooked, not brilliantly, but well enough. She shopped. She did some of the cleaning. She decorated the house. She indulged in all those small feminine actions that make a home.

Meanwhile, I was intent on being the man. What does the man do? He bets on horses. (I was a bookmaker's delight.) He hangs around with other men talking big. (I continued to spend time with my old friends in the old places—the racetrack, for example—instead of spending time with her at home.)

"Ava, honey, I'm gonna be a little late."

"But Mickey, I cooked something special."

"I know. I know. It'll keep. There are a couple of things I got to do."

"But hurry."

"Yeah, yeah. I'll hurry."

Once more a few days later:

"Ava, I got to work something out with the director. I'll be tied up."

"Again?"

"Ahh, baby. I'm sorry, baby. I got to do it. You understand."

"You better understand something, Mickey."

"What's that."

"Your supper is going to be cold."

And yet once more:

"Ava, I'm going to duck out to the track. I got a hell of a tip."

"I got a hell of a tip for you."

"What is it?"

"Stay home if you know what's good for you."

There came a day when Ava's belly hurt. "I think it's something serious, Mickey. It really hurts me."

"Lie down, honey. It'll go away." (I was busy figuring a parlay.)

"I tried lying down and it didn't help. It hurts, and the pain is on the right side."

"Yeah, I know how it is with those stomachaches." (The seven horse and maybe the three horse. That looks good.)

"I can't stand up, Mickey. It hurts me. Oooh."

"Well, maybe I better call a doctor." (Yeah, that's it. The seven and the three. Can't miss.)

I called a doctor who presently summoned a surgeon to remove Ava's appendix. (The seven horse won, but the three got beat a nose.)

The change of climate was so swift that neither of us realized what was happening. In quick succession we had been each other's date, each other's love, each other's spouse. From cool to hot in three turns of the dial. Now, still more swiftly, we became each other's sparring partner.

At one party—well, at many parties—I did my impersonations, told a few stories, tapped out trick dance steps, and played piano and sang. Ava, who could not impersonate, tell stories, dance trick steps, play piano, or sing, was condemned to sit in a corner looking beautiful. I suppose some women would settle for that, but it was too easy for Ava to look beautiful. She *was* beautiful. So she demanded more of herself and of those around her.

"Well, I thought you'd forgotten who I was," she announced at the end of this party.

"Mrs. Ava Gardner Rooney, beautiful lady."

"Can it, wise guy."

"What do you mean, can it? What did I do? Why the hell are you sore all of a sudden?"

"I mean, don't think a few words now are going to make up for the whole night. What did you do? What didn't you do? You were America's best entertainer, and America's worst escort."

"But, Ava, it was all for you."

"If you want to act for me, try acting the part of husband."

"Well, what the hell is a husband supposed to do?"

"Talk to his wife. That's a starter."

"Well, I'm talking to you now, Ava."

"Do me a favor."

"What, honey?"

"Shut up."

A few days later we went to the Palladium, as we'd done in the days before our marriage. I bustled in and someone said hello.

"Howrya, buddy," I said, walking over. "How's everything going down at the studio?"

"Fine and dandy, Mick. Say, you were great in your last picture. Just great, Mickey. I mean it."

"Thanks, pal."

"Say, Mick, there are a couple of people I want you to meet. Folks, this here's my friend Mickey Rooney."

"A real pleasure . . ."

"A privilege . . ."

"A great honor . . ."

A truckload of manure is what it was. But I was young and dumb and simple and stupid, and I looked around and there wasn't any Ava.

"Say, where's your wife tonight, Mr. Rooney?"

"Oh, she'll be with us in a minute."

She wasn't in a minute, or in an hour. She'd called a cab and gone home.

As I say, I didn't know what marriage was supposed to be, but this sure as hell wasn't it. Something was wrong. I thought about that for three or four days. Actually, I thought about that for ten seconds, but the seconds were spaced over three or four days. Then it was obvious. There was only one thing to do. Make that a triple bourbon, will ya, guy?

When I found our Stone Canyon house, Ava was waiting calmly. "Been drinking?" she began, like an old and patient wife.

"A cuppa drinks ish all."

"Good booze?" Ava asked, still under control.

"Shwell."

Ava picked up a full inkwell and threw it at my head. (A near miss, high and outside.) "You and the ink," Mrs. Rooney said. "A pair of spots on the rug." She wheeled and stalked from the room, her beautiful figure shimmering through her negligee. I was pretty drunk. I don't remember if I followed. Two will get you ten I didn't. You married guys will appreciate that.

Pregnancy terrified Ava. I don't know why. I don't think Ava knew why. I only know that when Ava was nineteen, the thought of having a baby filled her with nameless, unreasoning dread. (Was it the thought of having a replica of me?)

These things run deep. It is hard enough for me to examine myself, let alone examine the subconscious of my ex-wives. Perhaps Ava was afraid that pregnancy would spoil her physical beauty. Perhaps she was afraid of the pain of childbirth. Perhaps she was afraid that a child would impose too much responsibility on her. Perhaps, perhaps, perhaps. The motivations are less important than the fact. She didn't want kids. One night when our marriage exploded, it was this fact—terror, mingled with fury—that detonated Ava Rooney.

It began with a familiar scene: the party, myself on center stage and Ava in a corner. Then we were driving home and then we were upstairs. And the consummation that triggered a scene I'll never forget. It was when Ava eased herself out of bed and started toward the bathroom. As she walked away, I stared after her.

She had walked three or four steps, when she wheeled. I was lying back on a pillow and as she spun around in her nudity, I made a small sound of delight. Ava glared at me for a moment. Then, quite slowly, horribly clearly, she said, "Mickey, if I ever get pregnant, I'll kill you."

"Why, Ava? Why? What did I do? Why?" I heard myself calling these things, but even as I did, Ava was gone and I was calling at a bathroom door, closed and locked.

I call again twenty years later, I call again, "Why, Ava?" Maybe because she felt that out of that day's twenty-four hours, I had given her my undivided attention for only five minutes. Maybe because she was being hurt, as I was being hurt, by the collapsing marriage—and when Ava was hurt, she struck back. I tell myself these things now and they make sense. I tell myself, too, that from that dreadful night when Ava's feelings turned to hatred in the instant after love, our marriage was inevitably, inescapably doomed.

That's where it should have ended but didn't. It dragged on. Like one of those late TV shows, there was more to come.

If life were a movie, there would now be a dissolve. The scene would fade and when the screen came bright again, I'd have a new wife, and a new existence. But a hard thing about reality is that you have to live in between the dissolves. It isn't neat. It isn't easy. But you have to do it.

I did. I took Ava to Tijuana and she held my hand and pressed herself close to me and I hugged her and for all the world could see, we were a happy married couple. Then I got distracted by a colt and Ava called me a rotten bastard. Back in Hollywood, I took her out to dinner and we chitchatted cheerfully across the table. Then I stopped off for a few drinks solo and when I got home the living room looked as though the Bengal Lancers had ridden through, slashing. Ava had taken a knife and, in her fury, cut the furniture. She had been hurt. Her answer was to hurt me, symbolically (as the symbolists would say), by swinging a knife at something that I had bought.

The night we broke up, Ava said, "Get the hell out." It wasn't as dramatic as the night she threatened to kill me. It wasn't a particularly violent argument. She was complaining that I ignored her and I was saying, what the hell, I'm a public figure and I have to be available to my fans.

"Get the hell out."

"What?"

"Get the hell out of this house."

"If I get out, I won't come back."

"Good. Don't come back. I don't want you to come back. Now get the hell out of here."

I got, assuming that when I reached the door, she'd stop me. I reached the door. Silence. I walked out to the car, assuming that now she would come running. I started the car and raced it. The only thing running was the engine. I edged down the driveway slowly, so that Ava would have ample time to sprint from the house and flag me. Then I was off the driveway, in the street, looking back at a brightly lighted home, my home, from which I had just been evicted by one of the most beautiful women in the world. We had lived together for just eight months.

Something, of course, is missing. It's something that belongs in every honest account of a marriage. The something is a description of what the married life was like.

I know it's missing and there's nothing I can do about it. The description is missing because there is nothing to describe. Ava and I were married and we loved and we fought. Legally, this was a marriage. Actually, it was not. I was too busy dominating my world to invite Ava into it. She was too busy reacting to wait for me to mature. So I was I and she was she and after eight months of marriage we went our ways—me as me (but now having known failure), and she as she (but now having known marriage). Although we did not know it at the time, neither of us would ever again be as we were.

Nothing important is tidy. Not death, nor childbirth, nor the act of love, and certainly not divorce. My relationship with Ava, which began untidily, did not end with my driving off, forever fled from her life. It dragged on, sloppily.

I headed the car toward Densmore and the big house. "I'm going to have to stay here for a while," I told my folks. "Ava's a little sore."

"What happened?" my mother wanted to know.

"A fight, Mom. Nothing serious. It'll blow over."

I stayed around for a little while. Then I said, "Good night, Mom," and I went upstairs to my room and my old bed.

Alone, I felt worried but hardly distraught. I was Mickey Rooney, movie star, Mickey Rooney, big little lover. I'd never failed at anything. Could I fail at keeping a wife? Hell, no. A broad from the sticks, who could barely spell Hollywood. How could I lose her? It was ridiculous. Stupid. But if it was so ridiculous and so stupid, what the hell was I doing thinking about it? I'd buy her something. That would do it. What did she need? A mink. Yeah, a mink. Every girl goes nuts for mink. I'd buy her a mink the next day and be back in her arms the next night. There was nothing to worry about. So why the hell was I worrying? Face it, Mickey. You better face it. You aren't only married; you're in love.

I bought the mink and some jewels. It was a good mink, well worthy of Ava's beauty, possibly even worth the $10,000 it cost. I don't remember how much I invested in the jewels and in the other things I sent her.

"You know something?" I said to Sig Frohlich, one day.

"What's that?"

"It's more expensive to live away from a woman than to live with her."

"I guess so," Sig said. (I know so.)

I called Ava a few times, waiting for my gifts to warm her spirit. It was a three-week thaw. Then Ava said, "All right, Mickey. Come back home. This time we'll work it out better."

"Damn right we will, honey. Forget the dirty laundry. That's in the past. This time is for always, right?"

"Right."

It was a few hours before we fought again. We fought for a month or two and then our fighting and our life together were over. I formally moved out of Ava's life on January 15, 1943, one year and five days after the wedding ceremony at Ballard. The divorce was filed in May, and we were single.

I remember an item from Jimmie Fidler's gossip column about a pair of divorces. It began, "Two of the film colony's best known brides, Mrs. Mickey Rooney and Cobina Wright, Jr. (Mrs. Palmer Beaudette) . . ."

Even after marriage, Cobina Wright was Cobina Wright. Ava Gardner was only Mrs. Mickey Rooney.

They say to me, "See, she used you. She just wanted to borrow your name." And I say this: She didn't need my name. She made it as Ava Gardner on her own, first as an astonishing beauty and later, when dramatic coaches and life had jointly tutored her, as an actress. She made it on her own as Ava Gardner. Who the hell remembers Ava Rooney?

I remembered Ava Rooney. I couldn't seem to let her go.

I still remember Ava Rooney.

Losing her, failing at marriage, the quality of Ava's womanhood—whatever—had pinned me wriggling to a wall. Wriggling toward Ava and getting nowhere. She didn't want a fortune in the divorce. Compared to what other wives charged, Ava asked for a grubstake. No acrimony, as they say in the columns. Amicable. The acrimony was burned out in the marriage. After we were divorced, Ava seemed to be fond of me, and I loved Ava more than I ever had.

Now quite independent of Ava, I had high blood pressure. I'd flunked one Army physical because of it. As World War II dragged on, either standards or my blood pressure lowered. At any rate, early in 1944 I took another physical and passed. I'd been calling Ava from time to time. Now I called her again.

"Well, it's happened."

"What's happened, Mickey?"

"This is it. I'm going into the Army."

"Oh, Mickey. Oh, dear. How do you feel?"

"Lot of guys have gone in. I'm going in. No complaints, Ave. That's how I feel."

We talked some more, then Ava said, "Mickey?"

"Yes, darling."

"I'll wait for you, Mickey. When you come out of the Army, I'll be waiting."

Remember, this was long after our divorce. I couldn't believe my ears.

"I'll be waiting, Mickey." She'd said it again.

I don't know why Ava said it. Maybe she still loved me. Maybe she thought she did. Maybe she was upset. Maybe she just wanted to say something nice. But I went into service and was shipped to Fort Riley, Kansas, as a buck private, in fact the happiest buck private in the United States Army. I was the only private the Army had on lease from Ava Gardner.

This isn't the place for a discussion of the Army. I did better than some, worse than some, and when the time comes we'll get to it. But for me (as for most) the new life wasn't easy. It would have been even more difficult except for my memories of Ava. I wrote her long letters, long, passionate, and possibly mawkish. She wrote back warmly. She was still waiting. I wrote again. Her reply was brief. I wrote again. This time she didn't answer. I wrote and I wrote still again.

One night, after a hard day's march, I was lying on my bunk when someone shouted, "Rooney, they want you on long distance."

"Who the hell," I said, "is bothering me now?"

The telephone was in the dayroom of the barracks. I ran down. The phone was off the cradle. Outside there was one bare bulb, hanging from a wooden lamp post. There wasn't another light.

"Private Mickey Rooney?"

"Yes."

"Go ahead, ma'am."

"Mickey, this is Ava."

"How are you, honey? How are you Ave, baby."

"Mickey, I want you to stop writing to me. It's all over between us."

"What's that? What's that?"

"It's over, Mickey. Good-bye."

"Listen to me, Ava. I love you, Ava. Listen to me. I need—"

"Good-bye, Mickey," Ava said.

"Wait a minute. Ava . . ." I jabbered into the phone for a minute or two before I realized that the line was dead. To emphasize the finality of this last good-bye, Ava had hung up.

I started to cry. There was no one around, but it wouldn't have mattered if there were a regiment. I was a little guy in a big army who had just lost his girl. Down deep I knew. That's why I cried. I knew that after all the splits and reconciliations, Ava and I had come finally to the end of the road. I don't think tears are anything to be ashamed of.

I sat alone in the dayroom, the single naked bulb glaring at me from outside. The night was quiet. I sat alone and after a while I stopped crying and dragged myself back to the barracks and crawled into the bunk.

I lay on the bunk wide awake, remembering. My

thoughts were long and slow and deep and sad. But my revery was punctuated by intrusive elemental sounds made by the twenty or thirty strangers who were sleeping all around me.

II

There is a pattern to second marriages, a sort of pattern of replacement. When one marriage goes bad, a common, fundamental, almost universal reaction is to rush tail first into another. Why? To escape from loneliness, or to forget failure, or to restore a sense of order, or to possess a mate who reestablishes your equilibrium—or ego.

Divorce brings with it a period of shock. My marriage to Ava spent more time dying than living, but I still wasn't able to accept the end when it came. The shock of divorce is severe and often prolonged. After all, with the collapse of a relationship a certain number of dreams expire. A certain number of ideals die. A certain communication with another person is severed. I'd say that each time someone is divorced, a part of that person dies, just as whenever a child dies, part of the parents perishes as well. The divorced individual goes on, perhaps growing in sensitivity and understanding, perhaps becoming more mature, kinder, more thoughtful. Still, in the act of divorce something is murdered.

No one likes to die by inches. No one likes to dwell on the thought of his own death. Move on. Don't let terror weigh like a tombstone. What to do with death? Think of a life beyond, so say religions. What to do with divorce?

Think of another marriage, so say our psyches. Find a substitute for the first marriage, a substitute wife, a substitute life. Find a way to endure. Don't quit. Move on.

When Ava left, I felt a suffocating sense of failure. The old Mickey Rooney—the old, young Mickey Rooney who could never fail at anything—was dead. He was also in the Army, a long way from the yes-men and the back-slappers, the bookmakers and the bartenders who in Hollywood would have told him that Ava didn't matter.

How can anyone marry five times? I didn't marry five wives at once. I married them one at a time. Ava was a matter of intense love. Number two was going to be a matter of rebound.

While I was at Fort Riley, someone in California threatened my mother's life. As a public figure, one wins a lot of significant affection. But one is also a target for a small, frightening assortment of nuts and kooks.

We never found out whether the man who threatened my mother was a nut or a kook. He may have been both. But the situation was alarming enough for the Army to spring me for ten days. This was soon after the Ava breakup, and the ten-day leave was a little breathless. Like this: I flew to Hollywood, comforted my mother, talked to the police, met a girl, told myself I loved her, slept with her, told myself I'd marry her because who the hell needs Ava, thanked the police, and went back to Fort Riley.

Soon afterward I was shipped to Camp Seibert, near Birmingham, Alabama. There, jilting the new girl I'd met in Hollywood, I found a still newer girl. After an engagement that lasted seven days, I married her. I was going to marry the first girl who'd hold still. It was simple as that. Hell, as I look back on it, I'm lucky I didn't propose to my top sergeant.

Betty Jane Rase was Miss Birmingham of 1944. She came complete with mother. Betty Jane's mother, Lena, is now the operator of a successful motel. I helped finance it with the settlement I made in the divorce court.

During my brief stay at Camp Seibert, I managed to get three weekend passes. The first was to attend a special showing of my movie *Girl Crazy*. That weekend I met Betty Jane. The second pass was for our wedding. I forget what the third pass was for. Maybe a honeymoon.

I'm a little hazy about the courtship. In fact, I was a little hazy during the courtship. I'd been drinking.

Betty Jane was attractive, seventeen years old and Southern. I suppose this links her slightly to Ava, who, when we first met, was attractive, eighteen years old and Southern. But they were really very different people.

Courtship and wedding number two come back through the haze in which they were lived. The scenes return as kaleidoscopic pictures brief and blinding. Goodbye, Ava. Hello, K.P. Hollywood again. Flame. Darkness. K.P. Darkness. A big, gaudy brawl in Birmingham, Alabama. Now the sound track starts. Someone is making an introductory speech.

"Ladies and Gen'men. Y'all know who I'm introducing y'all to. Y'all seen his pictures. Y'all love him. Y'all know a grand little guy, Private Mickey Rooney!" (Cheers.)

I move to the mike. "How y'all." I turn away. "Psst, a little bourbon and branch." Back to the mike. "You saw my picture. It was a lot of fun making it. I hope it gave you as much fun as it gave me. You've been a wonderful audience." (Cheers.) Off mike again, "Hey, a little more bourbon, will ya please?"

Through the fog of a big room, crowded with drinkers, a major approaches. "Yes, sir, Major. How are you, sir?"

"Hiya, Mickey. There's somebody here who'd like to meet you." Adjacent to one golden oak leaf stands a girl.

"Well, hello there."

"Mickey, this is Betty Jane Rase. She's Miss Birmingham."

"Well, hello, Miss Birmingham. I'm Private Mickey Rooney."

"Oh, Mr. Rooney."

"Oh, Miss Birmingham. (Psst, a little more bourbon and branch.)"

Sometime that night I proposed.

"Will you marry me?"

"Yes."

"Well, whoddya know!"

What the hell, a poor start for a marriage that couldn't last—but which did produce two wonderful sons. Perhaps to each other, we were glamour. Who knows?

We were married a week later, on Sunday, September 30, 1944, in a routine ceremony at the major's house. On Monday, October 1, 1944, I was back at Camp Seibert in time for reveille.

I married Betty Jane because I was determined to

marry someone. I'd had some drinks, was hurt and lonely, reached and grabbed. Under other circumstances, it might have ended with the lunge. As things were, it had to end in marriage. I think the fact that Betty Jane was Miss Birmingham contributed, too. The best way to replace Ava, someone special, would be with someone else who was special. Betty Jane was special by acclamation— the prettiest in Birmingham, Alabama, in the year of Our Lord 1944. Thus, Mrs. Mickey Rooney, number two.

Why did Betty Jane marry me? Ask her. Maybe neither one of us knew then or know now.

About as soon as possible after the wedding ceremony, Betty Jane conceived Mickey Junior. Then I went overseas, vaguely pleased that a wife would be waiting for me to come back, unaware that when I did come back I would have to start living with her not only drunk but sober, not only during minutes of passion, but during the long days of my years.

If Betty Jane hadn't become pregnant, our marriage might never have been. It was instant marriage. It might have dissolved in instant divorce. Again, I specify that this is not the place for Army stories, but while I was overseas, I traveled 115,000 miles entertaining in the European Theater of Operations. I saw little danger and a lot of mud. Naturally, when I learned that Betty Jane was pregnant I was delighted. Overseas, in jeeps and on foot, in mess halls and tank ruts, the abstract thought of a wife and son sustained me. I was in love with the idea. I wanted everything to go perfectly. After Mickey Junior was born I arranged from Europe for a chartered plane to fly Betty Jane and the baby from Alabama to California. I don't know what it cost. I never thought about money in those days.

Betty Jane and Mickey moved into the big house on Densmore, and from time to time I got reports. Junior burped. Junior smiled. Junior turned over. Junior caught cold. Like some twelve million other guys in service, I wanted to get home. I was desperate to see my first son and second wife.

Ultimately, after a slow, hellish fraction of eternity, the war ended and I came back to America. Then my discharge. Then home. A fraction of eternity that had dragged.

My impatience, which at its mildest is severe, was ferocious by the time I got to Hollywood. My son, I thought. My own son. Will we get along? Will he like me? Maybe he'll want to be an actor. If he does, I can teach him. And I can teach him how to throw a pass and hit a baseball and serve a tennis ball. Maybe we'll be able to make some movies together. That would be something, wouldn't it? Starring Mickey Rooney and Mickey Rooney, Junior. A great idea.

As a matter of fact, Mickey Junior is now an excellent guitarist, but in 1945, at age one, he wasn't quite ready for show business. As I say, I get impatient. Anyway, I bustled home as if a buzz bomb was on my tail and started pounding on the door.

"Hey," I yelled. "Hey, Betty Jane. It's me. It's Mickey. Hey, Betty Jane. Hurry up. Open the door."

The door opened. Betty Jane said, "Hi." There I was staring right into her navel—Good God! had she grown.

I'll pass along a tip to any short man who is planning to marry a seventeen-year-old girl. Wait a couple of months. Every day make her stand up against the wall. Measure her. At seventeen, Betty Jane Rase was still growing. While I was in the Army, she grew four inches taller.

How about a little basketball, honey?

Well, I saw the baby. He was a combination of Shakespeare and Hercules. A genius and a strong man, obviously. Just give him a little time to grow up.

"How are you, B.J.?" I said, finally, to Mrs. Mickey Rooney No. 2. We were standing near the crib. It was a little tough for me to talk to her. I was moved by seeing the baby and besides, we were on different levels. Whenever I spoke, I was addressing B.J.'s stomach.

"Jes' fine," she said.

So you see, Betty Jane and I did have something to say to each other. We didn't have anything more to say, but we had something.

If B.J. had stayed short, the marriage might have been longer. But not much. We were strangers at our wedding and, except for the baby, we had nothing at all in common. In 1946, I made the final Hardy picture, *Love Laughs at Andy Hardy*. That year love—and life—were beginning to laugh at Mickey Rooney.

You don't quit. You certainly don't quit a marriage without trying. Wrong, I knew inside. So probably did

BeeJay. But we both tried. I bought a new $85,000 house in Encino, for Betty Jane and for Mickey Junior. I furnished the house. That's two tries. I suppose I gave up trying when, with the house bought, the furniture paid for, I found I had to live with Betty Jane.

I took her to parties, introduced her to my friends. She sat and listened and occasionally drawled a few words. We didn't fit. We were strangers. She bored me. Probably I bored her.

The truth is that I was still in love with Mrs. Artie Shaw. I hadn't heard from Ava, nor had I tried to reach her, since that phone call she made to Fort Riley. One thing I can do is take a hint. But I wanted Ava still!

Although I didn't know it, I had spun myself into a corner. Subconsciously I was carrying a torch for my first wife. I was unhappy with BeeJay and she was unhappy with me. Past and present were both working against me. I'd say I was in trouble.

"Mickey," Betty Jane said, "you never take me anywhere."

"I take you places. Stop complaining."

"You don't take me anywhere."

"I told you I do. Now stop it."

"You stop it."

"For Chrissakes, B.J., you started it."

"Well, why don't you take me anywhere? That's what I want to know."

"I don't take you anywhere because I don't feel like taking you anywhere. Isn't that reason enough?"

From me, silence. From B.J. anger. From neither one of us came tears.

Being an imperfect husband and knowing it, I decided we ought to have another child. I thought like so many (poor idiots) that children can help a bad marriage Timmy Rooney was born on January 10, 1947 and, like Mickey Junior, Timmy was cute from the beginning. I loved him. I loved both the boys. But, to be honest, I didn't love B.J. I suspect B.J. didn't love me. We could have had twenty sons, each one cute as can be, each one a wonderful boy, and it would not have mattered in the end. B.J. and I were ill-suited to each other. Not kids nor anything else could hide that fact.

I know, as you know, that marriage held together by children or for children is no marriage at all. I know that a marriage, invaded by tensions, hatreds, violences, can scar a child more seriously than divorce. I know it, you know it, maybe even Betty Jane knew it. But we had kids and we tried to keep our marriage going because that was the thing to do.

This happened to be a critical point in my career. Under good advice, I might have gone on without a slump. As we'll see later, the advice I got was bad. I was talked into leaving MGM, talked into a fight with Louis Mayer, talked into a business partnership that sapped my funds. I thought at the time that all these decisions were right. I never suspected the ruinous years ahead. But I felt tension. Things were happening. I could feel the stirrings of

change. I was troubled. Lord, I needed a strong understanding wife.

Could I turn to B.J. for support and counsel? No!
Could I ask Betty Jane about partnerships, agents, what
roles to take, what contracts to sign? No! Or I could have
asked, and she could have answered. But she couldn't
help make the right decision. She didn't have the background. So she was cut off from the vast areas of my life
capsuled in the word "career." She was cut off from everything that was important to me except my sons and my
physical needs.

When a man is troubled by his career and frustrated by
his marriage, he can do a lot of things. Drink. Channel his
frustration into works of art. Take the pipe. Or look for
other women to supply what he can't get from his wife. I
think most men go for the last. Kinsey thought so, too.
Adultery is one of the fruits of marriage gone to seed.

"Where were you last night, Mickey?"
"With Sig and some other guys, having a few laughs."
"You expect me to believe that?"
"Yeah, I expect you to believe that."
"Well, I don't."
"I don't give a damn what you believe."
No tears. Odd, isn't it? She didn't cry.

My life became a shuttle. I was commuting from post to
post. Bedposts. Sleeping around has gotten safer than it
once was. An Elizabethan hopping through London beds
could contract venereal disease or he could father an ille-
gitimate child. Nowadays it's changed (if you can smother

your feelings). Bedhopping has gotten safer. But one serious risk remains. A mature man sacking out with a lady may discover first that he enjoys the sack. Then he may enjoy the lady. In bed, a man's defenses are down. His guard and his attack are low. So, excited by sex he may fall in love, or believe that he has, which is the same thing. Now a bored lady, lying down in sport, is probably even more susceptible to the progression of quick sex— quick love. I'm not advocating chastity. But the fact is that profligacy, like anything else, has its peril. Myself, I ran all risks. I never thought to be afraid of love.

I spent some time with B.J., some time clucking over the children, and some time away from the house with other ladies. Home, except for moments with the children, was dull or abrasive. Inevitably, I found something better. I'm sorry I can't tell you her name. She is now happily married to someone else. Thank God!

Under the weight of frustration, I wrote some songs and tried to write some poetry. My new friend liked my songs, liked my poems, liked me. I wasn't quitting the marriage. I had tried. But I couldn't live with B.J. Although I was still married to her, I moved in with my new friend.

The side romance was brief and intense. One morning in bed, the lady said, "I'm going to leave you."

"You'll never leave me," I said. "You love me."

"Yes, I love you," she said, "and I'll probably always love you, but I'm getting married the day after tomorrow."

The day after tomorrow she got married. I got drunk.

Is there a point to this, besides the point that Betty Jane

and I were finished with something that had never begun?
I think so. I was serious about the other lady and I was
serious about being a father to my sons. I couldn't be
both. The lady saw me as a married man with two children. No future there. My preoccupation with her kept
me away from the boys. So out of an effort to be a good
father and a good lover, I was neither. Other people get
away with mistakes. I never do. I lost both the lady and
my sons.

In all my smugness, I didn't realize that loneliness can
sometimes cause the other party in the marriage contract
to seek surcease herself.

We have a double standard, right or wrong. A man,
chasing many ladies, is a *bon vivant*. A lady, caught by
many men, is a tramp. Whether the double standard is
good or bad, it exists. Whether we like to admit its existence or not, we are conditioned by it. Are and have
been. Consider some of the mores we live by:

A married man exerting his masculine rights is always
forgiven, a lady seeking new love (and a new life) is
condemned unless she is free.

The wife ignorant of her husband's affairs is sentimentalized as a wronged woman and robed in the cliché of
long-suffering wife. The husband ignorant of his wife's
search for new love is not sentimentalized at all. He
appears as a figure of mockery.

It's hard for a man to accept himself as someone who is
mocked. To me, accustomed to success and adulation,
such acceptance is impossible, or was.

One night, during a reconciliation with Betty Jane, a guest arrived. I believe he had been invited. Everything was dull in that house (except the kids). Betty Jane was dull, the life was dull, and the guests were dull.

After a few hours of tedious conversation, I'd had it. "Would you excuse me? I'm tired. I'm going to bed."

"Certainly," said my wife.

"Certainly," said the guest.

I tramped upstairs and tried to go to sleep. A few minutes passed. I couldn't find sleep. Instead I lay there thinking bitter thoughts. What the hell kind of movies was I making? Bombs. I better get back on the track. They told me to leave MGM. I was too big for any one studio. Go it alone. Well, so far going it alone was nothing. I'd have to find myself a decent part.

My thoughts shifted nearer home. What am I going to do about Betty Jane? I can stand her maybe four or five weeks at a time. Is that the way it's always going to be? Maybe, at least until the kids grow up, I'll try it that way. Stay with her as long as I can stand it. Then move out. Then come back. A lousy life for me—and for her—that's what it would be, but what the hell else could I do? I couldn't leave the kids. Hell. I'll never get to sleep.

I went downstairs for a drink of water. Then began the argument that was the finale.

Isn't it odd that this one time there were tears?

I got the hell out of there. I was four years late, but I got out. I'd been trying, telling myself not to quit for a long time. It was February of 1948, and I was out. I was out of marriage number two.

What about the boys? Mickey and Timmy, I don't see you much anymore. I'm sorry, boys, sorry you weren't born into a happier marriage, sorry I wasn't around more to father you, sorry so much of life was inflicted on you so soon.

I'm sorry, boys.

Go out into the world and knock 'em dead.

Your old man will be along to help you.

I let Betty Jane do the suing. It was a standard suit, vague and, like our marriage, dull, full of phrases like "irreconcilable marital differences." Before the divorce went to court our roles had been assigned. I was to be the loud, brash, impossible Mickey Rooney. Betty Jane was to be the victim.

It went about that way, except that the loud, brash Mickey Rooney didn't say much. Betty Jane did the talking. She complained about me to the judge and then she complained about me to reporters. "We had no home life," she told the press. "I never knew where he was. He was always out. When he was home, he called me names."

"Like what?" the press wanted to know.

"He called me a hick," Betty Jane said.

Her lawyer wasn't a hick. He was a city man—I think the town is Philadelphia. This is what I agreed to give in the settlement:

$12,500-a-year alimony for ten years.

$25,000 for a down payment on a new home for Betty Jane.

$750 a month as rent so that Betty Jane could move from Encino immediately.

$5,000 a year for child support.

One Mercury and one Chrysler.

How short are you, Mr. Rooney, since the last divorce?

Later, Betty Jane married again. Still later she was divorced again. She has again remarried. I wish her happiness. I was a lousy husband to her and she wasn't the greatest wife to me, but she's been a good mother to two wonderful sons.

I've relived the marriage many times. How much was her fault? How much was mine? I try to balance it. Dan, no matter how I weigh it, no matter what sort of scale I use, it comes up that nobody was right. We were both wrong, or at least, all the wrong isn't on my side. I began the marriage. Yes! Betty Jane ended it. I tried to use her to forget Ava, which was wrong, to provide me with something to come home to after the war. Betty Jane was willing to be that instrument. I was impatient with her in Hollywood and quickly bored. Betty Jane was boring. I strayed and chased around the town.

I have an obituary for my second marriage: Tied, Tried, Lied, Died. Betty Jane Rase Rooney, number two.

III

On the inside of the wedding ring I gave to Martha Vickers, Mrs. Mickey Rooney number three, this is inscribed:

Today, Tomorrow and Always: M.R. to M.R.

Someone who knew about the inscription reminded me of it while I was working on this book.

"Who's the other M.R.?" I said.

"Martha Rooney," he said.

"Oh," I said. "That's right."

You forget what you want to forget, don't you?

Martha Vickers. Mrs. Mickey Rooney, No. 3. Not Mrs. Mickey Rooney 3d. A difference of a few characters on a typewriter. A difference of worlds in life.

Every divorce hurts as every marriage begins with pleasure. Still, a second divorce hurts in its own special and unique way. After one, you tell yourself, what the hell, it wasn't me. The lady just didn't appreciate what she had. After two divorces, doubts begin to resound within the brain. Maybe it wasn't the ladies. Maybe it wasn't the circumstances. Maybe the trouble with my first two marriages was me!

The first marriage is a flight of innocence.

The second marriage is a flight of fancy.

The third marriage is a flight of desperation. (Damn, but this gimp-winged pelican is gonna make it, or bust his good wing trying!)

A lot of things closed in as my second marriage closed out. I broke up with a man named Sam Steifel, whom I had let plan my career. Good parts had become hard to come by. I could still get work. I've always been able to get some work. But I couldn't get much. There were hours, days and weeks when I was between engagements.

In fact, it was less a question of being between engagements than being between periods of unemployment. I wasn't broke, but I had to scramble to keep even. In the year 1938 I had starred in eight pictures. In the years 1948 and 1949 together, I starred in three.

One-third off. Get your Mickey Rooney, here. One third off.

I can't stand to be alone. I know about the uses of solitude. I know it's supposed to be good to get off by yourself and think. I know philosophers recommend periods of solitary contemplation. Well, let the philosophers contemplate alone. Myself, I always need a crowd.

It's easy to say, "You can't stand yourself. That's why you can't stand to be alone." Or, "You're insecure; you need the reassurance of company." Or, "When you're alone, you have to confront yourself and you are afraid of self-confrontation." Perhaps. Perhaps all of these things are true to a degree. The reasons are confused. The condition is clear. I love crowds and I despise solitude.

Hell is a rich garden of lemon and orange trees, and a field beyond, and a brook, and a mountain rising toward a robin's-egg-blue sky. Under the pale sky, amid the trees and rolling fields, to the horizon on all sides, there is no one. In the midst of fruitfulness and beauty, I am alone. Completely. Eternally. I walk in the garden of hell.

(Did I write that?)

Betty Jane was not a lot of things, but she was a barrier against solitude. With that marriage gone, I had a number of choices:

I could do what I'd done in Birmingham. Start drinking, find a pretty girl and count on my reputation and drive to get her to marry me before the last ice cube melted. But I didn't want that. One marriage of booze and impetuosity was enough.

I could try to go it alone. I could get my own place and live by myself as millions of bachelors do. Some are happy. Some aren't. Depends on the bachelor. But in truth, *I* couldn't really go it alone. I was twenty-eight; the horror of solitude was ground deep into me. It was rough enough moving away from my sons. Going against my natural inclinations at the same time would have pressed my endurance more than it could safely be pressed. I hated solitude in my best days. Why risk solitude now?

I could find a friend to room with me. From every angle this seemed like a sensible course. Friends can't collect alimony. The California community property law does not apply to friends. With a friend, I could have essential companionship and meanwhile look about for a new girl. Later if the friend and I split, it wouldn't cost me a fortune. Living with a friend seemed safest, smartest and best. I didn't rush from Betty Jane to Martha Vickers. When Betty Jane and I broke up I took an apartment with Jimmy Cook. Jimmy played saxophone. We had been in the Army together. Afterward he went to work for Harry James.

So you see, I'd learned a little. My career was in trouble, my marriage was gone and the quickest antidote in the world would have been to catch another beautiful lady. But I'd learned that antidotes can turn out to be poison. They aren't marked with a skull and crossbones. The dangerous antidotes for me are marked by a soft sweet face and rounded hips.

"How long is this setup going to last?" Jimmy Cook wanted to know.

"A long time," I said.

"You'll be married again in two months," Jimmy said.

"Not in two months," I said. "Maybe not ever."

Jimmy grinned. He didn't believe me, but as a matter of fact, I stayed single for a whole damn year.

I lived as a bachelor the way you'd expect a twenty-eight-year-old bachelor to live. I chased. Sometimes I caught the quarry. Sometimes she got away. I was trying, like most young bachelors, to sleep with every pretty girl in the universe.

Young bachelors of the world, attention! Stop trying. You can't do it. There'll always be one more pretty girl to catch. Always. And all of a sudden you'll find out you're not young anymore. You'll find you're tired.

Set yourself a cutoff point, men. Accept the fact that you can't have every girl in the universe. Set yourself a cutoff point, say 5,000 girls. You'll find that after the first thousand gals, you'll be ready to settle down. (Provided that the thousand and first girl you see doesn't have a sweet soft face and rounded hips.)

My bachelor life included dinner parties. At one party in 1949, I found myself feeling particularly discouraged. All my chasing had done little for me, except my legs were getting stronger. The career was really sagging. I was tired. I'd been tired before, but now, at twenty-nine, I felt a new kind of fatigue. I mean it wasn't something that a few hours of sleep would shake. It was a fatigue that endured. Of course it endured. I was depressed. The fatigue was born not of years, not of work, but of depression.

There were movie people at this particular party. I don't remember who many of them were because I settled down with one. She was Martha Vickers, beautiful, auburn-haired and 5 foot 3½.

We started talking. "You're drinking a lot," Martha said.

"Yeah. I guess I am."

"You shouldn't really. You have so much talent."

"Thanks, Martha. Thanks. Talent and troubles. That's what I got."

"I know, Mickey. I've been divorced myself."

"Yeah. I knew the guy. A nice feller."

"It just didn't work and when a marriage goes bad, everybody gets depressed."

"I've had two marriages go bad on me. That's twice as depressing, Martha."

"You have to be patient with yourself, Mickey. Don't ride yourself. You have a lot of talent. You have to protect it."

Martha was a successful actress on her own; perhaps her best picture was *The Big Sleep*. She knew the Hollywood scene and she knew divorce. She was sympathetic (and beautiful). I began to feel a little less tired.

"What do you think makes a marriage go bad?" I said.

"I don't know. A lot of things. If I did know, maybe my first one would have stuck."

"Did you blame yourself?"

"Of course, Mickey. Everybody does."

We talked a little more and I began to tell Martha things about myself. We sat sipping Scotch. I talked. She listened. Kindly.

It's surprising when you stop and think about it. Already, Hollywood—certain people in Hollywood—were turning against me. I don't mean this in a paranoiac way. I don't mean a proclamation went out: Get Mickey Rooney. But during my heedless early years, I had made an imposing list of resenters and enemies. Some disliked me for my success. Some disliked me for my wives. Some disliked me simply for myself, perhaps deservedly so.

When I was No. 1 at the box office, these people had to keep their feelings to themselves. Hollywood—the community in which I traveled—was a one-industry town. I was a big man in that industry. The pattern is the same anywhere. If you work for I.B.M. and you dislike a vice-president, you keep it to yourself. But when the vice-president starts to slip, as I had started to slip professionally, you can afford to talk. Maybe at I.B.M. they talk like this: Why the hell does he always wear blue ties? He keeps pinching that secretary and she won't let *me* pinch her. Look at all the money he's making. I could do his job ten times better. He's a son of a bitch. The company ought to can him.

Talk goes much the same way in Hollywood. Rooney's

too loud, too brash, too rich. He drinks too much. He dates too many beautiful women. All thought but not expressed aloud when I was hot. Now, when I was tepid, they came creeping out from under rocks on Mulholland and Ventura and Sunset and Hollywood and Vine. They came creeping out and they said, "Rooney's no good. Never has been. Never will be. He's washed up."

I don't rage about people who dislike me and let me know it. Then the lines are drawn, sharp and clear. What bothers me are friends, or perhaps acquaintances, who in rough times turn out to be non-acquaintances. I'm going to write a song about their approach. You probably know the melody:

> *Should non-acquaintance be forgot*
> *And never brought to mind*
> *Should non-acquaintance be forgot*
> *Or kicked in their behind?*

A lot of people were busy forgetting Mickey Rooney. Others were busy kicking him in the vital spots. But here, I told myself as I sat with Martha Vickers at the party, was a beautiful, successful lady who didn't want to forget me, didn't want to kick me. She actually seemed to give a damn.

"They're turning on me, Martha," I said.

"Who?"

"Everybody. The studios. The agents. You know what my last two pictures were? *Summer Holiday. Words and Music.* Where are the parts like Puck? Who the hell killed

Andy Hardy? What's going on in this town, Martha? Why are they all turning on me?"

"You mustn't turn on yourself, Mickey. *Everybody* isn't turning on you. How old are you?"

"Going on thirty."

"You talk as though you were going on eighty. You shouldn't give up or be bitter. You're too talented."

A hand was reaching into my limbo. Martha's hand. She was compassionate and ladylike and gentle. She was worried about me, worried about my career, even worried about my drinking. Worried about my drinking! Later on our home was to seem like a New York bar the night before they put in prohibition.

I married them one at a time, and each satisfied some overwhelming need. Ava, the first love. Betty Jane, the Ava replacement. Martha, the hand into limbo. I needed them all. Not now. But then. And always, before my mind, the cursed horror of loneliness.

My romance with Martha was the slowest and most careful yet. I wanted it that way and so did Martha, perhaps even more strongly. I had been twice burned. She had been once burned. We didn't have too much skin to give away.

"Do you think it's us?" she asked one night.

"What do you mean?"

"I mean about the marriages."

"No, it isn't us. A couple of bad breaks. Three bad breaks. Two for me and one for you."

Kiss.

"Can I hit the top again, Mart?" I asked another night.

"Sure you can."

"But all these enemies, all these people who get so much pleasure saying I'm through."

"You can overcome them, Mickey."

"How?"

"With talent and understanding."

Kiss.

"Could we make it together?" I asked, a little later on in our relationship.

"I don't know yet, Mickey. I think we should be very careful. I don't want to do anything that would hurt me—or you."

Kiss.

The moments in public were at different restaurants and at a few pleasant bars. The moments alone were the kind that led to caring. Martha showed me her home in North Hollywood. She introduced me to her parents, Frances and Ted. Quietly (for me) we drifted into love.

"I want a church wedding," Martha said one day.

For a long time, I couldn't find a church that would marry us. I spoke to three, four, half a dozen ministers. "I'm sorry, Mr. Rooney. I don't think our church would be suitable to your needs." Or, "Terribly sorry, but I'm afraid we can't help you, much as we'd like to, of course." Or just plain NO!

"It has to be a church wedding, Mart?"

"Yes. I want everything to be right."

"Well, churches don't want to marry us."

"Why not?"

"The divorces, maybe. Or me. They never say. They just talk nonsense. I tell you, Mart, it makes me wonder what a Christian church is. I mean, sure we made mistakes, but isn't Christianity supposed to be a religion of forgiveness? 'Father, forgive them. They know not what they do.'"

Finally, a minister at the Unity Church in North Hollywood consented to marry us. I'll always be grateful to him and to his church. A matter of demonstrating that there is more to Christianity than words, that Christianity is indeed what it purports to be, even if some of its exponents have forgotten or never have known its true intent of truth and love.

We had gone out together for five months when we were married. The date was June 3, 1949. As Martha wanted, everything was right. A church wedding. A June wedding. Everything.

"This one," Sig Frohlich predicted, "is going to stick."

"I know it will," I said.

And so it did—for two years.

Everything was right, except this: We were married.

I bought a modest house on White Oak in Encino. The town of Encino seems to have a magnetism for me. I guess Encino is the closest thing I have to a hometown and our living there was by choice. I didn't buy a modest house by choice. My career was slumping and besides, Betty Jane had tapped my till. When I married Martha, I wasn't poor, but I was far from wealthy.

Unhappily, my third marriage coincided with a curious divorce. It was my divorce from the community of Hollywood. That estrangement is a story, in fact a chapter, in itself, but it is important that I mention it here. Isolation from Hollywood within Hollywood was the background against which Martha and I tried to make our marriage work. My old gang was pretty well broken up. The old Hollywood establishment was dying off. The new establishment had no place for me. Partly through my own mistakes, I was so far outside I could barely see in.

As it happened, the marriage didn't work. Neither did I.

I don't know what Martha expected of me. Probably she believed that after we married, my career would pick up and we would then live a normally busy life. A customary feminine reaction. "Oh, he's having trouble now, but when I get my hands on him, I'll straighten him out. All he needs is the right girl."

And who *is* the right girl?

Martha!

I don't know what I needed. The right representation and the right outlook were two things. At that time I had neither. A girl, at least a girl like Martha, was not enough to suffice.

We set up our home and now she was Mrs. Martha Rooney and I was off on marriage number three, but the hell of it was that nothing really changed. We were living together. We were man and wife. But my career still worsened. I'd been depressed and I stayed depressed, only now with a new wife in a new house. Double depression. Depression for two. Come live with me and be depressed. Togetherness.

"They won't let me work, honey."

"Keep after them. They'll let you work."

"Well, they sure won't let me work today."

"Then what are you going to do today?"

"Have a drink."

"Make me one, too, honey!"

"Martha, how am I going to keep on?"

"Keep on what? You're not doing anything."

"That's it. I mean keep on working. Keep my career moving."

"I don't know, Mickey. I'm not an agent."

"Okay. Okay. Let's have a drink."

"The town's against me, Mart."

"Yes. I remember. You've told me. The town's against you. Nobody loves you. Nobody wants you to work."

"It's true."

"Well, I want you to work."

"Huh?"

"Get behind the bar."

"Maybe I oughta quit the business."

"Maybe. Yeah. Maybe you oughta quit the business."

"What the hell kind of a thing is that to say?"

"You said it first."

"Well, it's one thing for me to say it, but to hear it from my own wife. It makes me want to take a drink."

"Make one for me, honey!"

It wasn't always toddy time. Occasionally it was bedtime. Teddy, my third son, was born a year and a half after our marriage. By the time Teddy arrived, the relationship had slipped badly. It was beyond salvation, even by the arrival of God's greatest gift, a child.

The marriage to Ava had ended in turmoil. The marriage to Betty Jane had ended in shock. The marriage to Martha simply ran down, like a toy whose spring had worn out. The marriage ran down and there was that boredom, ennui. There are a lot of words, including incompatibility.

At first Martha had been my consoler. Then she grew tired of consoling me, tired and perhaps resentful, and perhaps confused. She married me with many excellent intentions but with one mistaken view. She would help me for a time, hold my hand, pat my head, and *presto*, she thought, I'd re-emerge as popular as Andy Hardy. Hers was a normal drive for a wife. A good, understandable, admirable drive. After a little hand-holding and head-patting, I still remained an actor who was usually unemployed. This was my failure—nobody's but mine. But my failure, interwoven with Martha's failure to remake me, turned both of us away from each other, and eventually turned us toward drink. For a time we were alcoholically overboard. Martha would sit around and blot up my troubles (plus Scotch). I'd sit around and blot up hers (plus gin). After a while all our talk turned aimless. Then, inevitably, it turned sharp. When this happened—and it did before Teddy was born—the marriage was wrecked and we were strangers together in a living room, strangers together in a kitchen, strangers together in a bed. Legally man and wife, but legally only.

For all her caution, poor beautiful Martha didn't know what she was getting into, marrying me. During our engagement, her warm phrases and her presence were sufficient to comfort me. During our marriage I needed a depth which she was unable to supply. A depth and a passion. (God, Ava. Why? Why?)

So I knew. I knew with horror and fear and disgust. Another marriage was crumbling away under me. She wasn't right for what I needed. Had I been more success- ful, had I been working, I might not have noticed. As it was, there was so much time, so many needs I wanted her to fill, that I *had* to notice. I drank and she drank and everything went blurry, except the fact that no drink could blot out. We both knew. We were wrong, the wedding was wrong. To one bad marriage, she had added another. To two bad marriages, I had added a third.

The divorce was filed on June 11, 1951. I agreed to pay $150 a month toward Teddy's support and a descending scale of alimony that began at $2,000 a month.

I paid when and what I could.

Now years later the paying is all over. Mart and I are

friends. Maybe we should have stayed just friends, but if
we had, there would be no Teddy.

It was worth it.

This divorce bowled me over. I didn't want to see
anybody or talk to anybody. I was ashamed of myself
again. There wasn't any excuse for failing at three marriages. There wasn't any excuse for scattering children
around town. There wasn't any excuse. I was ashamed. So
ashamed of the me that was and the me that wasn't.
Except, why the hell get on myself? It took two to make
the marriages and it took two to make the divorces.
Martha reacting to my disorder with a disorder of her
own. Martha clutching for something that I couldn't give
her. Martha finally unresponsive. What the hell, did she
figure I'd come back big and they'd all say, "That Martha,
there's a great girl. Look what she did for miserable
Mickey Rooney. A great girl, like Lincoln's mother or
Madam Curie or something." That, I thought in my senseless bitterness, must have been what she wanted. But—
still senseless, bitter—what right had she to demand me to
be something I wasn't? Except, again, I was demanding
something, too. Be actress, princess, psychologist, wife,
studio chief and mistress all in one. And she wasn't, and
what kind of an idiot was I after two marriages to stumble
into something like that? Why did I always trap myself?
Why couldn't I stay with one woman? There was something wrong with all of them, plenty wrong with all of
them, but I couldn't keep puffing on the private pipe for-

ever. I had to face it. There must be plenty wrong with me. That was it! But *what* was it.

"Sig, I gotta get out of this lousy town and you gotta come with me."

"Okay, Mick. Okay. Take it easy."

"How the hell can I take it easy? They won't let me work. Now another divorce. You gotta come along, and get some sleeping pills, kid. I've been having terrible insomnia."

With Sig Frohlich, I went to the Shamrock Hotel in Houston, Texas, for no reason I can remember. It was a big splashy hotel, which didn't make a damn bit of difference to me. I was leaving big splashy Hollywood. I didn't want girls or excitement or people. I wanted to hide from girls, excitement *and* people. Most of all I wanted to hide from *myself*.

We checked in, I went to bed and took a fair number of sleeping pills. Not enough to end it. The thought of suicide never entered my mind. But enough to postpone it. Oh, Christ, I had to get away, get under that blanket of sleep where they couldn't hurt me and I couldn't hear them or feel them, the broads and the operators and the children, my children, far away. I had to get out of this world for a while and get under, get under, get under so goddam far that they'd never find me and I'd never find myself.

"Sig."

"Yeah, Mick."

"Don't go 'way, pal."

"I'm going nowhere, Mick. I'm stickin'."

"Thanks, Sig. Thanks, pal. Don't go 'way. Please don't go 'way."

Mercifully, came my night.

We stayed at the Shamrock for more than two weeks— the only two weeks of my life that I have ever devoted to an absolute escape from life. Twelve or fourteen hours after gulping my first handful of pills, I awoke a little bit. Not very much at first. Just enough to remember who I was.

"Sig. Where's the pills?"

"Hey, Mick. Take it easy, will ya?"

"I know what I'm doing."

"Mick, ya just woke up. Don't you think you oughta eat?"

"I know what I'm doing. Where's the pills, Sig?"

"You've had enough pills."

"Sig. Don't argue. I know a doctor who told me things, like how many of these pills I can take without dying. Now, for God's sake, gimme the pills."

"I'm not gonna do it."

"Sig, goddammit, goddamn you, I ain't gonna die from the pills. I'm gonna die if you make me stay awake. Goddammit. Goddamn you, Sig. Please, Sig. The pills!"

Poor Sig. Poor Martha. But not, dammit, poor me.

I went to sleep again.

I guess—I know—that sometime in the two weeks I must have eaten food and drunk water. But not a lot and not often. I was getting under, the way I wanted, getting far, far under, under everything. That was what I wanted and that was what I was working at. Pills. Sleep. Wake. Please, Sig. Pills. Pills. My merciful night.

You see what I mean about divorce? It doesn't get easier. But jokes. You have to make jokes.

I wish I could tell you more about the two weeks at the Shamrock. They're probably a particularly significant part of my story. But what is there to say? I slept for two weeks. *And when I waked, I cried to dream again.*

Then one day in Houston I announced, "I'm through sleeping, Sig. It's all right now. Let's go home. How long we been here?"

"Two weeks, Mick."

Sig's loyalty to me, now in its second decade, had been rewarded in the way that meant most to him. I was going back to face Hollywood and possibly, just maybe, myself. I can't explain the roots of such loyalty. No one can. One can only be grateful.

"You got any plans?" Sig wanted to know.

"No," I said. "Nothing. Nothing at all."

"Well, don't get married tomorrow," he said.

"Not tomorrow or ever, Sig. Don't worry."

I went back and set up bachelor quarters, not with Sig but with another friend, Don "Red" Barry, who'd been in pictures, and I liked the bachelor life so much that I didn't marry again until November of 1952. Almost two years a bachelor—my record as a man.

. . .

I dated a stripper, a nice girl who suffered from five o'clock shadow. I also played Korea, which, as you'll see later, was one of the bright periods of my career. Korea and golf, that was what I played. The pictures by this time had titles like *Sound Off* and *The Strip*. The American public was not clamoring for my work. But the men liked me in Korea. And liked or not, one thing I could always do was hit a golf shot. It was while hitting a golf shot—or just afterwards—that I first saw the long, inviting legs of the lady who was to become my fourth wife.

IV

I try not to be bitter about Ava and B.J. and Mart, and, at least in my calmer moments, I succeed. Look, I tell myself, Ava was a kid and B.J. didn't know what she was getting involved with and Martha meant well. No knocks. I don't mean that sometimes I don't feel a surge of hostility toward any or all of them. But generally, with these three former Mrs. Mickey Rooneys, everything is under control.

It was harder to keep hostility under control when I thought of the fourth Mrs. Rooney. Why? She didn't serve me badly. In fact, she tried very hard to be not only wife, but secretary, bookkeeper and accountant. But it was the bad fortune of Mrs. Mickey Rooney number four to marry me when everything was at an ebb. My career was shot. My attitude was dreadful. My consistent handmaiden was despair. Those were bitter years, and angry, while we were married. They left me with a bitter kind of hangover. While still getting over that, I felt somewhat bitter toward Elaine. That's wrong—but there it is.

This was a marriage that lasted for almost seven years. It could, I suppose, be compared to The Seven Years' War.

Elaine Mahnken was cool, willowy and redheaded. I first saw her in 1952, a year during which I made only one picture, and so had as you can imagine a surplus of free time. One day I took my free time with me to a driving range on Ventura Boulevard and, looking up from a topped drive, I saw Elaine's legs. I topped a few more, then offered to help her with her swing. She accepted my offer. The lessons began at once.

Although divorce never gets easier, proposing does. By the time I met Elaine, I knew all the moves. I'd made them three times before.

I proposed very quickly. Elaine talked about love. "You can learn to love me later," I said.

"Well, I don't know if it's that easy," Elaine said.

Ha, ha.

Elaine, a highly female lady, understood the uses of reluctance. She stood me off for a while, then said one night, "You better stop proposing, Mickey. I might take you up on it."

"I dare you."

An hour later we were flying to Las Vegas in a chartered plane. In Vegas, at the Wee Kirk of the Heather, we were married on November 18, 1952.

Elaine's attractions were beauty, understanding and, it

was to develop later, a friendly father. I liked Fred Mahnken the first time I met him. I liked him for a long time
after that. He was alive. He loved racetracks. He
gambled, as I did, and he admired me (as I had once done
but no longer could). The town of Hollywood was against
me in 1952, I thought. Friends were vanishing. In marrying Elaine, I added one wife and one new friend.

It may sound preposterous. As it ended up, it was
preposterous. But I was down and sinking deeper. My
roots were in a town that didn't want me. The ladies I had
married were all fled. My children were growing up in
strange houses. Why should I, a three-time loser, marry
once again? Why not take a long time? Why not take
stock?

Because it hurt too much. That's why. Because they'd
stripped off the skin and stripped off the muscle, and now
my bones were showing. I was deep in self-pity, sure, but
think of it like this: I was in quicksand. I saw a beautiful
girl and later a man, her father, on the high ground.

"Help. Please. Throw me a rope."

So I was married. Mrs. Elaine Mahnken Rooney. Mrs.
Mickey Rooney number four.

Rope burn?

It didn't hurt at first.

I wrote something one black night. It's where I was
when I married Elaine. It goes like this:

Where would you like your life served, sir? In the drawing
room or on the terrace? Or perhaps picnic style, replete with

arm and arm reflections beside some mirrored lake? No, we'll have a buffet and invite the world. Only one condition. Eat all you take. And as for the soiled and garbaged dishes, we'll leave those to be cleansed by the future.

Does that make any sense to you? Is it any good?
It's what I felt then, the best that I could express it.

I bought a huge house on Fryman Road, in Studio City, a few miles up the Freeway from Encino. I don't know how I financed the house. I must have found a banker who was a fan of Andy Hardy's. Buying the place took almost all the cash I had, and made me carry a mortgage that I couldn't afford. Foolish, but when you marry a girl and she wants something very much, you try to get it for her. Your manhood seems to be at stake. Here I was slumping, spending money faster than I was earning it, and here was this girl, my fourth wife, my first redheaded wife, making her first real request. So it was important that I grant it. It was important to her, important to our relationship and important to my own self-respect. Some-where, somehow, the money materialized. Buying that house, I felt I was doing the right thing.

There was one problem with our lavish home. It had to be furnished. And there was one problem with buying furniture. The money for furniture was invested in the home itself. When we first moved in, our furniture con-sisted of two mattresses: a large one for Elaine and myself and a small one for Elaine's father Fred. (After a while, we scrounged up enough cash for furniture. We had to.

We went on Ed Murrow's *Person-to-Person* and we couldn't do that sitting on orange crates.

Such problems are surmountable. We weren't the first couple with more house than we could furnish. Nor were we the last. But there were other problems, mine and hers, that were too much for us. First, Elaine's drive for material things. She had been a poor girl. For a time she had worked as a carhop to support herself and her parents. For all the time that she was my wife, she was, I believe, possessed by a fear of returning to poverty. I was not her breadwinner, but her cakewinner. With icing. The second problem was Elaine's first marriage. It was all over with legally. It was not all done with in her own mind.

Elaine's first husband was different from me in at least two ways. He was 1) tall and he was 2) handsome. I don't know whether it was that Elaine wasn't entirely through with him, or whether it was that he wasn't entirely through with Elaine, but there was some kind of slap between them over our marriage.

One story is that after the marriage, he felt I would end up hurting Elaine. Another is that after we got married, he felt I would grubstake Elaine. That story ends up with his asking Elaine to ask me for a loan.

I don't know. I prefer to think that both stories are absurd. At any rate, Elaine's first husband died mysteriously not too long after she and I were married.

Fred Mahnken, Elaine's father, was, I thought, a helluva guy. "I want you working for me, Fred," I told him.

Fred said he didn't want charity.

"It isn't charity," I said. "I want you around."

"No, kid, it's charity," he said.

"Look," I said, "I got this big house and all these grounds and I can't take care of the whole thing myself. Suppose you do it for me. Be the handyman. Take care of the gardening. I'd have to hire a handyman and a gardener, anyway."

"I don't know if I can," Fred said.

"Sure you can," I told him. "You take care of the place and I'll give you a check from time to time. Not charity. You'll work for it. You'll be doing me a favor."

"Well, as long as I'm doing you a favor, all right," Fred said.

I wanted to help Fred out and I did, but I've got to add this. It's not always a smart idea to hire in-laws. (Hello, there, Hollywood!)

There was an atmosphere about Elaine which I did not detect early. It was the atmosphere of tragedy. People who courted Elaine's deep love also seemed to court disaster. The first husband had died. I had nothing but trouble during our seven years. (I was nothing but trouble for seven years.) I think her continuing relationship with her first husband is interesting.

About two weeks after we were married, I got a phone call with what I took for gossip. It was someone I knew. I forget who exactly. He said he was calling to tell me that he had seen my new wife with a man who looked like her old beau. He had seen them together in close conversation, and in close quarters. Who needs lying rumormongers?

"I don't want to hear talk like that," I said.

I didn't want to hear it, but I *had* heard it. After a while I heard more, from Elaine.

"You know I was married before."

"Sure. I know."

"Well, there's nothing between us. We went bust at the divorce. You know that. I love you. But he's in a terrible mess and he can use some help."

I knew she'd been married before, but in the hot haste of my move toward Elaine, I hadn't learned much more. The first husband, it seemed, was in trouble. Elaine wasn't quite sure what kind of trouble. Probably a gambling debt, she thought. So would I be a good guy and help this good guy who was in trouble?

"No."

"What do you mean, No?"

"I mean No."

"He's a good guy, and he needs your help."

"My help? Where do you get *my* help? I didn't marry him. I don't even know him. What the hell's going on?"

"It's the only decent thing to do."

"Forget it."

After that, was our marriage ever the same?

If it was not bright, it was at least a marriage, something to which we both clung with desperate, irrational passion. I was profoundly afraid of divorce and whenever a thought of tearing this marriage struck, memories of previous divorces overwhelmed me. Elaine was, I believe, deeply afraid of poverty. So, each with a fear, we clung to the marriage as we clung to each other, desperately, passionately, irrationally. And as we clung, I learned more of Elaine.

Elaine had a strong ambition to become an actress. Once, before marrying me, she had modeled for a calendar. That's one way to crack movies. Before posing for something that might be hung in barberships all over Los Angeles, Elaine decided she needed a disguise. She finally found the disguise. It was a blond wig. She wanted to act and she thought that since she'd posed for a calendar, maybe I could help find her parts.

I agreed to that. I decided to direct her as a character in a television series, based on the life of Daniel Boone. (This was long before Disney's characterization.) It wasn't a bad idea. That was the trouble. It was a good idea for the TV business, which had gotten rich on bad ideas. It didn't sell. If Elaine wanted to crack show business, and she did, she had picked a poor agent in me. I could seldom work myself, let alone hustle for my wife on the side.

Elaine also had a lust for the outdoors. She liked all sports, as I was to learn, but among her diverse interests were horseback riding, boating and fresh air.

"I like sports myself, Elaine. Golf, tennis. You know. But face it. I'm *not* a woodsman. That Daniel Boone thing was for television, not real life."

"How do you know you don't like the outdoors, when you haven't tried?"

"Well, I've tried enough to know I'm a city guy. Did I ever tell you about the time I broke my leg? That was outdoors."

"I get so cooped up in the city," Elaine said.

Cooped up in a lavish house, I thought angrily. Before you married me your whole home was barely as big as our living room. I thought that, but didn't say it.

"Maybe we could get a country place," Elaine said, "where we could get away."

"If we buy a country place, we won't be able to get away anywhere."

"Why not?"

"Creditors."

"Then let's get something cheaper. Let's get a boat."

"Yeah, yeah. But not the *Queen Mary*."

"Oh no, Mickey, darling. Just a little boat. Just a nice little boat. It'll be wonderful, Mickey, darling."

"Yeah, yeah, Elaine. C'mere."

I bought a big, expensive cruiser, with the help of another friendly banker. I was making a bit of money from pictures and making some more playing club dates. With some effort, I was able to make the down payment. But that was all. Nothing left for frills, such as insurance.

We docked the boat in a marina near Santa Monica. It had been caulked, as all boats are, but whoever caulked my cruiser was no caulker. He was a plumber, expert at opening clogged drains. On the side, he built spillways or he practiced urology. What I mean is, his speciality was letting water through.

I made friends with some of the men at the marina. I showed them the boat, where everything was, where I'd stowed the liquor. Late one night, a few weeks after I'd bought the boat, I got a call from one of my marina friends.

I can't quite reproduce his speech. For a few minutes he told me about my liquor. It was excellent liquor, he said.

Then he mentioned the boat. There seemed to be some trouble.

"What's the matter?" I said, wide awake. "Someone steal it?"

No, nobody had stolen it.

"Then what the hell are you bothering me for at this hour?"

It took a long time, but finally I understood. The boat had been leaking. Now it was listing. (That's why I can't reproduce his speech. When a drunk says "listing," he sounds as though his tongue has been replaced by a half pound of bubble gum.)

"Come on," I told Elaine, and we went like hell. We reached the marina soon enough to see the top of the boat. All the rest of it was submerged. The men explained that when my boat started to sink, they had hurried to rescue my liquor. Rescuing led to sampling. Now I had no booze, no boat (and no insurance).

"Let's buy another boat, Mick!"

Was all Elaine ever said to me, "Let's buy"?

Of course not. Elaine made any number of efforts to

say, "Let's save!" She took over the books when we got married. She tried to work out some kind of a budget. She wasn't frugal, but she did try. I give her this. Just about every time she had a budget that was balanced, I'd go out and unbalance it for months. She tried.

I bought another boat as Elaine urged. This boat came with house attached. Elaine was terribly depressed by the city, she said. She simply had to get outdoors. So I bought her a place in the great outdoors. The place I bought was at Lake Arrowhead, a resort in Southern California which is not very far from Los Angeles but which lies high in the mountains. The waters of Lake Arrowhead are blue and clear. The shoreline grows thick with evergreens. It is beautiful for a resort and for resorting.

"Honey, I think we ought to have more than a house, you know," Elaine said.

"I know what?"

"You know. Other things."

I'd bought her a motorboat for Lake Arrowhead. "You've got two houses, a boat and a Chrysler," I said. "You've got other things."

"Well, would it be all right if I bought some horses?"

"No, dammit, it would not be all right."

"Just two horses, Mick. One for you and one for me."

"I'd rather bet 'em than ride 'em, Elaine."

"Horses aren't expensive."

"Maybe not if you ride 'em."

"Well?"

"No. No. No!" I said with finality.

A few days later I bought the horses.

My career at this time—the '50's—consisted of some work in bad pictures, some work in television and some work at clubs. But as the '50's passed, I was beginning to earn a living again. There wasn't too much time for me to go to the place at Arrowhead. Besides, I liked Hollywood better.

"Mick, I think I'll go to Arrowhead for a few days."

"I can't go. Forget it."

"That's all right. I'll just go by myself."

"It's not all right. Stay around here."

"Oh, baby, you're always working and all that, and you won't miss me if I go for a few days." She moved in, in her cool, arousing way. "You won't even miss me, and if you do, I'll give you something to remember."

I missed her. But more and more Elaine stayed at Arrowhead, offering me a series of explanations. I was preoccupied with righting my career. I was away a lot myself. When I was home, I spent a lot of time at the track. It wasn't as if I needed her all the time. She got depressed sitting in the big house waiting for me, wondering where I was. It made her happy to be out in the woods alone. It made her happy and I could get together with her there whenever I wanted, or if it was important, she could come back to town in a few hours. So this way, we'd both be happy. I was married to Elaine but I was spending most of my time with her father.

It was plainly a troubled marriage. I had my orbit, she

had hers and the orbits seldom overlapped. But the terror of divorce stayed strong and I stayed with the fourth Mrs. Rooney. She stayed with me as mistress of two homes, two horses, one car and one motorboat and, her relatives.

I heard stories. You always hear stories, particularly if you've been married four times. People seem anxious to tell you, "Hey, buddy, No. 4 is on the rocks, too." They tell you that out of a strange fascination. They want to watch you react. "We might as well tip off the little guy, and see if he goes all to pieces. Come along and bring your friends. There isn't any charge. Come along and watch Mickey Rooney disintegrate."

I had, of course, talked divorce to Elaine, but only in moments of anger. I had, at times when she seemed more intent on being away from me than being with me, ranted. "I don't know why I ever married you. I picked you up and your father, too. I picked all of ya up. I don't know why. I oughta get the hell out, get a divorce."

Elaine was usually cool. "Again?" she'd say.

More angry, I'd rant on. Divorce. Escape. Relief. Ranting and rancor. Elaine was bleeding me dry. She wanted to live like the wife of a movie star, which is a reasonable dream. But hell, she'd married me and I was an ex-movie star. Certainly I wasn't much of a star in the mid-'50's. That, Elaine could not accept, or would not accept. So she drove on, drove herself and drove me and drove through my money, and I should have gotten out as quickly as I'd gotten in, but I couldn't. I could talk divorce—but I didn't want to be alone.

Maybe there's a whole other marriage here. Maybe

there is all that Elaine meant our relationship to be. I mean she wanted to make the marriage work. And then, as I guess she must have seen it, I was ducking out for emotional relief—with booze, pills and—face it, I'm no virgin—other women. I know at one point she got an accountant, not for herself but for us. I know that at times she wanted to make sure every bill was paid. I remember one night when she had all that was left of our bills in an envelope. She wrote a few checks, then held the envelope upside down to show me that it was now empty.

"We don't have any more debts," she said.

"Great."

A few weeks later, at the crap tables of Vegas, I got us in debt again, this time for keeps.

I wasn't much of a husband after a while. I looked for God knows what. She looked for companionship. After a long time, nothing is neat.

Now is the time for all good men to get another divorce. Elaine's first husband was dead. Our marriage was dead. Elaine told newspapermen that I didn't love her anymore, and that the reporters ought to look for me to seek a divorce. The newspapermen, doing their job, printed the stories.

Elaine was right. I didn't love her anymore. Our marriage dragged on for seven years and my love had lasted for about two weeks—until she'd hit me for the loan to her ex. She might have rekindled the love if she'd cared to, if she'd worked at it. Or maybe I could have done the same. But no, she had her ways—horses, boats, money-spending—and I had mine, and it was too bad, really too bad that we didn't get along better, but that was about all there was to say. Too bad. Then, restless, we roamed. And so the marriage was destroyed.

I was luckier than Elaine. After our separation, I met Barbara Thomason. This was like coming to the perfect end of an imperfect journey. Here was a real love. Here was a love to be seized and more than that, to be kept. I had to get a divorce quickly, I knew.

To be quick, it had to be clean, and to be clean, it had to mollify Elaine. She insisted that the divorce occur in the state of California. Then she went through two lawyers, looking for the right case. The later Jerry Giesler then dropped her because she was asking too much. She found someone else and this is what he got for her from me:

The house in Studio City.

The house in Lake Arrowhead.

All the furniture.

The motorboat.

The Chrysler.

The horses.

Assorted jewelry.

Five thousand dollars cash.

My agreement to pay her $21,000 a year for ten years.

Elaine Mahnken Rooney, number four. Divorce filed February 5, 1959. The obituary is a long, loud, clear scream of pain.

. . .

While the divorce was being negotiated, Elaine talked to Barbara once. She'd called me at dinnertime and Barbara, cooking for me, answered the phone. "Get off the phone and get Mickey," Elaine said. "I have to talk to him about the settlement."

"Why?" Barbara asked.

"I have to straighten out my life."

"What about Mickey's life?"

"I said I have to straighten out *my* life. Put Mickey on."

Rage. Hate. Bitterness. Mine and hers. You seldom get divorced out of love.

In court, Elaine said that our home life was disorganized and that I didn't like her cooking. Apparently, that really bothered her. Some time after I'd married Barbara, Elaine invited me to join her for a chicken dinner. "I'm cooking a real good chicken," she said.

If I'd gone, I would probably have been mailed a bill. And for two chickens, at that.

Jokes. I hope Elaine can crack some about me.

V

I sit now in a house warm with children—Barbara and I have four—and touch my bald spot and wonder how. How? Why? What did I do, or fail to do? What special lust, what strangling dream, what desperate needs have moved me? I sit and I think, looking at the lemon tree in the garden.

Begin, then, as we all begin, as children. Begin then

with a child in need of love, a child who, in the unreality of acting, finds perfect love bestowed on him by strangers.

A young man. A stirring in the loins. Miss Ava Gardner. Ava here at my side and Ava fled both in an instant of memory.

A beauty queen. Bad luck. (Bad luck.)

An actress, offering her hand to lead me. Lost both. Dissolution in solutions of Scotch and water. No longer young. No longer loved.

Comes a poor girl. Beauty comes again. Beauty must always come. Bad luck. Bad luck. Bad lust.

So Mrs. Mickey Rooneys, there you are, one through four, and I sit in the house warm with children, I sit watching the lemon tree and asking why. I know a few things; not many but a few.

About myself, there is this terrible need for affection, this terrible terror of solitude. Marriage satisfies the need and quells the fear. I am more naturally inclined to marry than most. I seem to need a wife more. Since I had money and fame, I was immediately desirable. I could marry beautiful women. Could marry them, needed to, and did.

But marriage must do more than satisfy a need and quell a fear. It must do more than answer problems. It must create things new, things different, things exciting. Through the first four marriages, I was never able to find a creative relationship with a wife. And, of course, that much was bad.

But this is good: I have been fearless in my fight for happiness. I haven't quit and said, well, what the hell, it isn't much, but I'll make do. I've gone on, dying a little with each divorce but still going on, still taking marriage seriously, still adoring women. I have been set back sometimes but I have not been willing to live my days in an unquiet limbo. I have known fears and miseries beyond what many know, but these things, these unsuccessful marriages, were part of striving. The striving was reckless. I wish it hadn't been. But deeply and endlessly I am glad I strived.

The women I wed, did they move on from me to happiness? The record says that they did not. They've sputtered about, even as I. At worst, I lit their wicks, but they've been sputtering. I found women who were as troubled as I and if the psychologists want to say I did that unconsciously, I'll concede this: When I proposed to Ava I was almost unconscious with passion, when I proposed to Betty Jane I was almost unconscious with booze, when I proposed to Martha I was almost unconscious with despair, and when I proposed to Elaine I was almost unconscious period.

To the best of my self-knowledge, under the unassailable banner of truth, I tell you I have married often because I have searched for perfect love.

Thus I am. Thus let me be. Till death.

6 * Grab Bag

I

The obstetrician who delivered Mickey Junior sent me a bill for $5,000. I paid it. Promptly. Then, for delivering Timmy, he charged me $5,000 again. Betty Jane picked her doctor and I've wondered at times whether she was getting a kickback. But no. Two babies. Ten thousand dollars. Special delivery.

The surgeon who removed Ava's appendix charged me a flat $10,000. A remarkable abdomen, and maybe a remarkable appendix, but this man was performing double surgery. He operated on Ava's body and my bank-roll simultaneously.

Everybody grabs. When you're a movie star, extrava-gantly famous, presumably rich, everybody wants to grab a slice. The doctors want to be Robin Hood. "The reason I'm charging so much, Mr. Rooney, is that it gives me a chance to work for free among the poor."

"Poor? I thought you practiced in Beverly Hills."

"Well, what I mean is that someday, when I do practice among the poor, this $10,000 will help."

"Okay, okay. Can I give you a lift, Doctor?"

"Sure. Would you mind dropping me at Santa Anita?"

(Lots of poor people out there.)

Everybody walks up, palms high. Doctors, lawyers, caddies, managers, bellhops, false friends, fifth cousins, former wives, and doormen. They huddle. All right, gang. We got a movie star here. He's live. He's primed. We go with play Triple Zero. You remember play Triple Zero. It's the old Grabarooney.

I'm a sucker for the Grabarooney. I have been for years. They've run it to the right of me, to the left of me and sometimes they've run it straight over my skull. I'd come up muddy, bloody, but I'm game. I'd wipe the mud from my eyeballs, the blood from my wallet. Ready? Here it comes again. The old Grabarooney. More mud, more blood. I guess I better buy a new wallet.

Where does the Grabarooney end? I used to wonder. I wondered, but I never knew. I never even guessed. When I found out, one sunlit morning in the late spring of 1962, it was a grinding shock. I was seated in Los Angeles bankruptcy court. My assets were $1,500. My liabilities were $346,513.12. Shall we say that again, slowly? Three hundred forty-six thousand, five hundred thirteen dollars and twelve cents. My liabilities.

The old Grabarooney. They grabbed and grabbed and grabbed. Then all of a sudden they ran out of Rooney.

As closely as I can estimate, I've earned about $12 million in my lifetime. I don't suppose that has too much meaning. Place 12 million singles end to end and you could carpet the Appalachian Trail. Pile them and you have the Green Mountains. But the issue is not placing them or piling them. The issue is spending $12 million. How can anyone bust a roll like that?

People have theories. It's the wives, some guess. The ladies cleaned me. Like some of my wives, that theory can withstand anything but analysis. I haven't paid $12 million in alimony and child support during my lifetime. I haven't come close. A take of $12 million should get you through twenty-four marriages, picking some of the most expensive women in the world. The four former Mrs. Rooneys have not gone begging for mink, but we're talking about millions here, not thousands.

Others suggest that I've gambled away all my money. Well, I've gambled away part of it—$165,000 in a single, destructive year—but only part. If I sat at a dice table day and night for ten years, I'd be hard put to drop $12 million. I don't say I couldn't do it. Just that I'd be hard put.

The truth of course is that I haven't done it. Again the point is: A thousand is different from a million.

Taxes? They're fierce and when you fall behind, as I did, they become fiercer than anything you've known. But I haven't paid $12 million in taxes. As I understand the Internal Revenue laws, no one is ever expected to pay more than he earns. It seems that you are, sometimes, but only seems. I can't blame taxes. Everybody else pays them too.

That leaves bad business deals, handouts, extravagance and slashed pockets to account for the rest of my money. I've had experiences with all.

But it isn't as if my bankruptcy can be traced to any single cause, placed in any single period of years, explained with a single flip phrase. My wives have been complicated. My finances have been complicated. The hell of it is, all I want to do is entertain. The hell of it is in all this financial complexity I'm a simple (if not a simple-minded) guy.

An actor acts. If he's a bad actor, it ends there. "The guests are waiting in the parlor, sir," he mumbles. Exit, and presently the bad actor is punching cash registers in a supermarket.

When a good actor acts, his act or craft is only the beginning. It is the essential beginning. Without it, nothing else matters. But his performance is like the top of an iceberg. You see it, and it's impressive. You don't see everything underneath.

An actor, however good he may be, needs an agent to find him roles and to negotiate contracts. Then he may also need a personal manager. The manager looks for roles, negotiates contracts and watches the agent. Finally, the actor needs a lawyer. The lawyer watches the manager watching the agent.

An actor acts, but he is also a property, like *Three acres, two-bedroom house, pool, view, $125,000, Pacific Palisades*. The actor concentrates on his acting. The others concentrate on him as a property. Without good people around him, an actor may go out of business. There are thousands of actors around and it is easy for producers to forget. A good agent and a good manager do not let producers forget. In exchange, they won a piece of the property.

I'll tell you about money. It's like this. Stanley Kramer wanted me to play a role in his comedy *It's a Mad, Mad, Mad, Mad World*. He wanted four months of my time and offered $100,000. That's $25,000 a month, or just twice the salary of the President of the United States. A fortune? Here's what happened to that $100,000 during those four months. We'll take off the top, which figures. Everybody else did too.

Salary	$100,000
Agent's Commission (10 percent)	10,000
	90,000
Manager's Commission (10 percent)	10,000
	80,000
U. S. and California back taxes	25,000
	55,000
U. S. and California current taxes	30,000
	25,000
Lawyer, accountant and secretary	6,000
	19,000
Sig Frohlich (for helping me perform)	3,500
	15,500
Mrs. Rooney No. 4 (Elaine)	2,400
	13,100
Child support to Mrs. Rooney No. 3 (Martha)	600
	12,500
Child support to Mrs. Rooney No. 2 (Betty Jane)	1,800
	10,700
Business expenses at $500 a month	2,000
	8,700

There it is. How to turn $100,000 into $2,000 a month, with a bit of extra change in my pockets. I work for four months, earn $100,000 and get to keep $8,700. Out of the $8,700 comes living expenses—food, clothing, medical bills, and the rent. $100,000 equals $8,700. Rooney's Law of Economics.

And still I hear, "You must be rich, Mr. Rooney. After all, you earn big dough." I'm not knocking $8,700. What I'm knocking is the missing $91,300.

II

I started going bankrupt when I was fifteen months old, which is when I started working. It has to begin there. It has to begin there and move on to a child somewhat older awakening to a curious fact. What he liked to do—entertain—brought him money.

I half forget the child. It was so long ago. But half-forgotten, half-remembered, the child named Joe Yule, Junior, must have found a funny thing. What he was doing onstage, he did because he wanted to and because his mother wanted him to and the people beyond the lights (who were applauding) wanted him to. He was paid, but that didn't matter much. He was enjoying himself. That was important. And the funny thing was that for enjoying himself, people paid him. That must have been a funny thing to think of. Do what you want and the man will give you money.

There are grown-up terms such as thrift, economic stability, fiscal responsibility. They don't apply at all.

When I was a child and we needed money, I did what I liked and the money came. Money was never important then. It isn't now. I like the things, some of the things, that money can buy. But that isn't saying I like money.

I didn't need agents or managers or lawyers until I got to Hollywood. In burlesque, the business of acting was pretty simple.

"We'll give you and your wife and the kid forty bucks a week, Joe."

"Okay," my father, Joe Yule, Sr., would say.

End business.

(The best agent in the world could have negotiated that offer all the way up to $41.50.)

Hollywood was different. Thirty-five years ago, I was a hardworking pupil at Daddy Mac's Dancing School on Hollywood Boulevard. I practiced tap routines and a bit of acting. On weekends Daddy Mac rounded up a squabble of children, herded them into cars and shipped them collect to Orange County, near Los Angeles. There we staged shows at little theaters. Not much; just enough to separate the promising children from the ones who stammered.

My first agent found me at Daddy Mac's. His name was Harry Weber and he was experienced, honest and fair. Harry Weber steered me through the Mickey McGuire days, nudging my salary upward as quickly as he could. It never got very high; $125 a week was about all. But Harry did what he could. No complaints.

A few years after signing me, Weber became ill and sold my contract to Frank Orsatti, a robust, round, bubbly man. The price was $2,500 and Orsatti began recouping his investment immediately. He brought me to MGM. There, as you know, my salary reached $5,000 a week, plus bonuses, before my twenty-first birthday.

In everything Orsatti and Weber did I had an additional agent, working free. The agent was a judge provided by the People of California. As I've explained before, under what's usually called the Coogan Law, after Jackie Coogan, any child working in the movie industry is protected by the California courts. This guards him from wicked stepmothers, as in fairy tales. A judge reviews each contract to see that it is fair and, if possible, makes sure that some money is locked away in a trust fund. My early contracts provided for two trust funds, one for myself and one for my mother. I think each trust fund reached $150,000.

A lot of good work was done for me by Weber, Orsatti and later by an agent named Johnny Hyde. They worked legally, and successfully and so did the California judges over periods of weeks and months and years. Then, with terrifying swiftness, the good work came undone, like a noose tied by a pacifist.

Shortly before entering the Army, I met an intense, bespectacled Philadelphian named Samuel H. Steifel. He liked my acting, Samuel Steifel did. Once at a charity auction in Philadelphia, he'd bought a pair of drumsticks I had used. At first he seemed to be a fan. Then when I was having Ava trouble, he seemed to be a friend. We all became friends; my mother, Sam Steifel and I.

Steifel had grown wealthy operating a chain of theaters in Baltimore. He walked about with a pocket bulging green. Apparently, he liked to lend me money. Made him feel important, I supposed. Anyway, I liked to borrow.

"Come on, kid," Sam would say. "Let's forget Ava. We're going out to the track."

"How're you doing?" he said one day, after four races.

"I'm not. Damn number four horse cut mine off. My jockey didn't look like he was trying."

"Want to recoup?"

"No, Sam. I don't want to recoup. I'd rather lose. That's what I came out here for. To be a loser."

Sam reached into the green bulge, pulled a roll of hundreds, counted five and gave them to me. "Sure that's enough?"

"That's enough."

"Take some more."

I took some more. I was so busy borrowing, I didn't notice Sam making small significant marks in a little book.

Why did I borrow? Well, nobody ever brings enough money to the racetrack to cover a bad day. I had bad days. And also, it didn't seem like borrowing. We were buddies, Sam and I. Or rather Sam was my buddy. His buddy was the little book.

My mother, like most mothers, was shaken when her boy went into the Army. Probably she was shaken more than most. Her only son, who had meant so much to her, who had been so successful, was suddenly transported from her life. There was money, but much of it was tied up in trust funds. A big chunk of my mother's security vanished when I put on khaki.

Good old Sam. He cheered my mother by lending her

money. All the time I was in service, he visited her with his big green bulge. When I got out of the Army in 1945, I discovered that the Rooney family now owed Samuel H. Steifel something over $100,000.

There wasn't any easy way to pay him back. A lot of the money I'd made was still locked in the trusts. My savings had dwindled while I was in service. I was not poor, not hungry, not hard-up. I just didn't happen to have a spare $100,000.

"Don't worry about the money, kid," Sam Steifel said. "What's a hundred grand between friends. You forget about the money. There's just one thing."

"What's that?"

"From now on, I'm your partner."

"What's that?"

"I'll run your career for you. It'll take off."

"Okay," I said. "Fine, Sam."

"And we're in this 50–50, Mickey. Whatever you make, we split."

Steifel took advantage of a lightheaded kid, myself. I should probably have been plowing my money into real estate or stocks, instead of into the racetrack. So I can forgive Sam for getting hold of me. I wasn't a baby, although I acted like one. I mean he took me, but who the hell can be a promoter without a sucker? Sam was the promoter. I was the sucker. I don't blame Sam. I blame the sucker.

I don't forgive his maneuverings with my mother. I try to forgive my debtors. I even try to forgive my creditors. But there are limits.

. . .

Steifel got a lawyer and the three of us set up a company called Mickey Rooney Enterprises. Sam owned half of Mickey Rooney Enterprises. He was going to deduct my debt from the profits. Who owned the other half of Mickey Rooney Enterprises? Oddly enough, Mickey Rooney.

Now we had a company. Next we rented an office, a big plush suite on Sunset Strip. There I had a large desk and a pretty secretary and I could play the businessman. I was a puppet really. I knew nothing about being a businessman. I'd never even acted the role. But Sam pulled the strings and since he knew me, my temper, my intensity, he had me dancing to his satisfaction and my own.

Right after World War II, Campbell Soups had wanted me to star in a radio series. The deal fell through. Another radio contract was offered. Somehow, this collapsed too.

"Look," Samuel Steifel, partner in Mickey Rooney Enterprises, told me one day on Sunset Strip. You simply have to get into radio."

"Why?"

"You're getting too old to play juveniles in pictures. I told you your career would take off, but we gotta get it moving. We gotta get you into radio."

"Doing what?" I asked.

"Playing Andy Hardy," Steifel said.

It wasn't a bad idea. If I looked too old for Andy, I didn't sound too old. If I watched the booze, skipped the whiskey basso, I could carry a teen-age voice into my sixties. "Helluvan idea," I told Steifel.

"Right, Mickey. All we gotta do is clear it."

Metro-Goldwyn-Mayer owned Andy Hardy and the way to clear something at Metro was to talk to Mayer. Steifel, the lawyer and I made an appointment and a few days later set out for Mayer's office.

To see L. B., you had to pass a line of pretty girls at typewriters. They weren't secretaries. They were secretaries to secretaries. Then some more girls. Real secretaries. Finally you walked into an office big enough for a game of touch football.

Mayer was always changing his office décor. He had the room decorated every four weeks. Some days it looked like a palace. Some days it looked like a steam room. Some days it even looked like an office. On the day Steifel, the lawyer and I marched in, it looked like the Ross Ice Cap. I mean it was white. The desk was white and the rug was white and the walls were white and the furniture was white.

Mayer was behind the desk. "Sit down, Mickey. Good to see you, boy. Hello, Sam." This was the friendly voice of L. B. Mayer, the friendly tyrant.

"How are you, L. B.?" I said.

"Fine, and you're looking fine yourself. I've always taken a great personal interest in you. It makes me happy to see you looking so fine."

"Thanks, L. B."

Steifel ended the small talk. "We'd like to put the Hardy series on radio, Mr. Mayer. It's a chance for Mickey to make another score for himself."

Mayer glowered, said nothing.

"And, of course," Steifel said, quickly, "the studio will get full credit and a royalty."

Mayer's glower softened. He turned toward me. "Mickey," he said, "you know I'd like to help you. I've always liked to help you. You're one of my favorite boys, Mickey. And a great actor. Anybody comes in here, tries to tell me Mickey Rooney isn't a great actor, I shut him up. And quick."

"Thanks, L. B."

Mayer resumed as though I had not spoken. "But you understand show business, Mickey. That's one of the things I like about you. You understand the business. So you understand that an Andy Hardy radio show might detract from the value of the pictures. You know I like you, Mickey, and I'd like to help you, but you see I can't say yes, Mickey. I have to say no, you can't put the series on radio."

"Then from now on," I said, "you can get Butch Jenkins to play Andy Hardy."

"I'll throw you right out of this office," said Louis B. Mayer, my friend. "I'll throw you right out of here on your head."

"Maybe you could have done that before I went into the Army," I said, "but not now."

He didn't say anything, didn't make a move. "I'm walking out of this office," I said, "and all I can say to you is 'luck.' "

I'd liked Louis B. Mayer for a long time and, in his way, he'd liked me too. Then, in a single instant of double rage,

I understood the nature of our relationship. I was a nice little fella and as long as I stayed a nice little fella, L. B. would continue to like me. If I played horses, or chased a girl, he understood. He understood either very well. And neither mattered because I did my work and my pictures made money. I was a nice little fella whose Andy Hardy pictures made $75 million for Metro. "So he makes a little fuss. What he makes a lot is money."

As I sat in the big white office, so intent on cracking radio, so hurt at being turned down, it suddenly struck me that over all the years, Mayer had been thinking of Metro. Well, it was time for someone to start thinking of me. That thinking went into the brief, harsh line: "You can get Butch Jenkins to play Andy Hardy."

Hollywood was run by the studios and Metro was the biggest studio in Hollywood. And Louis B. Mayer was Metro. I had now antagonized the most powerful man at the most powerful studio in Hollywood. The next move was logical, if distasteful. I should apologize.

Did my advisers suggest that I call L. B. and say I was sorry about my temper? They did not. They told me I was as big as MGM.

If my career had a turning point, it was here. Currently, Elizabeth Taylor or Cary Grant can tell off a studio head safely. That's because these days the studios are scrambling to survive. But I'm not talking about these days, I'm talking about the days just after World War II. In those days no one could tell off a studio head safely. I told Mayer off rashly, which was only the beginning.

"I think," Sam Steifel said later, "we ought to leave MGM."

"Yeah," the lawyer said. "That's a good idea. We ought to."

The "we" was me.

"We'll make pictures on our own," Steifel said. "We'll make a settlement with Metro and start an independent company. That way you'll get what you should, Mickey. That way, you'll make real money."

As long as I worked for Metro, I was on salary. That salary went into Mickey Rooney Enterprises and we could then add to it, if we chose, by marketing Mickey Rooney T-shirts, Mickey Rooney's Greasy Kid stuff and Mickey Rooney's Own Patented Love Potion. We didn't choose. But the primary income, my income as an actor, was almost entirely straight salary. By starting an independent company, I could have added a lot more. Instead of throwing a salary into Mickey Rooney Enterprises, I'd be throwing in the profits from a picture. You don't have to know any more high finance than I do to know that profits are the name of the game. Would you rather have the salary of the president of American Telephone and Telegraph, or the profits the corporation makes? Sam Steifel would rather have had the profits. The hitch, as I learned, is there first must be profits before the partners can share them.

Steifel owned half the property, which was me. He wanted to improve the property, make it grow. I wasn't getting any taller, so what Steifel finally urged was a deal that might help him and could ruin me.

The idea of starting my own company appealed to my ego. I was angry at Mayer. I'd show him and the studio. I was bigger than all of them. I'd be the first Hollywood star to beat a studio, I'd tell them off and make them come around begging.

Only one man warned me. Fred Pankey, my stepfather, is an accountant, and he handled the books for Mickey Rooney Enterprises. Day after day he warned me to make peace with MGM. Day after day Steifel puffed up my ego; I was bigger than MGM. An actor can't exist without ego. I listened to Steifel and he and the lawyer negotiated my release from MGM.

Ultimately, the one to blame is myself. Ultimately, I can't fault Steifel or a lawyer or anyone else for the bad deals I've made. They negotiated deals, but I approved what they negotiated. Ultimately, the man to blame for Mickey Rooney's leaving MGM is, of course, Mickey Rooney.

But in the years that followed, restless, difficult years, I had plenty of time to look back on what I'd abandoned. At Steifel's urging but on my own responsibility; this is what I gave up:

1. An MGM contract that paid me $125,000 a picture. (Remember, this was in 1946, when $125,000 was about twice what it is now.)

2. A pension plan which would have covered me if I had stayed at MGM for four more years. Under that pension, I was to have received $49,000 a year at retirement age.

3. The tremendously powerful publicity machine operated by MGM. My press clippings were never better than when MGM was keeping the reporters happy.

4. The General Motors of the movie business.

This chapter is money. This chapter is balance sheets. Let's look at what I got in exchange:

1. Sam Steifel, an operator, short on talent.

2. A crutch for my ego.

How come you make such sharp business deals, Mr. Rooney?

Well, secretly I'm a financial wizard.

What are the guideposts for your business deals?

Rocks. Within my head.

For all Louis B. Mayer's desire to throw me out of his office, he was not about to throw me out of the studio. I mean he might have tried to throw me toward the big white door for free. But if I wanted to get out of my contract, that was something else. That wasn't free. My contract was valuable. I'd have to buy my way out.

Steifel then set about buying what he called my freedom. (Lord, I was well off as a slave.) For emancipation, I had to agree to make five more pictures for Metro, at $25,000—not $125,000—each. The missing $500,000 was to complete payment for my contract. Of the $25,000, $2,500 would have to go to my agent, Johnny Hyde of the William Morris Company, and $12,500 would have to go to Steifel, under our agreement. That meant that I'd be paid $10,000 a picture. Star in three movies a year and I'd earn $30,000.

Rocks. Within my head.

I'm weak at arithmetic. I don't understand. If my contract was worth half a million dollars, how come I was only worth $10,000 a picture?

The wheels that I'd ride to bankruptcy court had begun to turn.

As you probably know, many stars have formed their own production companies in recent years. The reason is as plain as one of those letters that orders: "Bring all records. Don't leave the country. This is an audit, bud." The reason is the tax structure.

Steifel's basic idea—independent productions—had merit even then. He saw it as a way for him to make money. I saw it as a way to pioneer. But there was too much going against me. First, MGM had a call on my services. Then Sam Steifel had never produced a movie in his life. I was tied up by the terms of my release and Steifel had to learn the movie business. A hell of a way to start.

Often Steifel told me he was close to making a deal for a Mickey Rooney Enterprises Production. Close? Everybody in Hollywood is always close. A girl gets off the bus from Butte, meets a slick young man and the last thing she hears is, "You'll be in pictures tomorrow, honey." The old story. Close.

Steifel was always close and how many movies do you

think we made? Think small. Think tiny. Think nothing. Mickey Rooney Enterprises never made a movie. The great partnership of Rooney and Steifel made a total of zero (0) movies. That was the kind of production company we had. A better Hollywood hand than Steifel could have set up a good many pictures for me in those days, but if Steifel were a good hand he wouldn't have come to me through my mother, would he? He wouldn't have had to.

While Sam stayed close to nothing, I had to work for MGM. My blowup had angered the studio and there was no great effort there to find great pictures for me. "What are we gonna do with this stinker, Wilbur?"

"Cast Rooney in it. That is, if you're sure it's a stinker."

I had to work for Metro. This was preferable to night court, though the difference may not have been easily discernible.

I made *The Big Wheel* for $10,000. If you saw it, you're in a small, unselect minority.

I made *Quicksand* for another $10,000. As a few hundred critics wrote, I sank in the stuff.

I was making a third bomb when Fred Pankey finally got to me.

"I don't know what Steifel is spending," Fred said. "He won't let me look at the books."

"The son of a bitch," I said.

"Mickey," Fred said, soft and earnest, "if you ever got out of anything in your life, get out of this deal."

We were sitting in my office at Mickey Rooney Enterprises. "We're getting out of here right now," I said.

"Great," Fred said.

We walked outside without looking back. But at what cost and after how many years had slipped through my fingers like gems?

III

Samuel H. Steifel is dead. He used to tell anyone who'd listen that he'd never gotten square with the Rooney family. Maybe not. I don't remember all the terms of our split. But I know one thing. Sam Steifel got even.

In the three or four years that he ran my career he milked me for what he could, which was bad enough. But after we split, I almost had no career, which was worse. This chapter is about money, but I'm no accountant. I can't say exactly what Steifel cost me. Still, add up what he took, what he tried to take, the Metro settlement, miscellaneous other sour advice and you'll have a pretty good sum. Maybe even $346,513.12, or what I owed the day I went bankrupt.

Free of Steifel, I had to return to Metro, fingering my hat. I had to go back to the studio that was bigger than Mickey Rooney. I would have apologized to Louis Mayer, still fingering that hat, but Mayer was gone from the vast office, gone in fact from the studio. Hollywood was changing swiftly. In Mayer's place, as emperor of a declining empire, sat a sharp-faced man named Dore Schary.

I'm not a fan of Dore Schary's. I know he's written *Sunrise at Campobello* and done some other things, but

I'm not his fan. He took over Metro and decided, for reasons of his own, that the star system was outdated. Whether it was Schary's ego or simply his business judgment, I don't know. But Schary broke the star system of the studio that advertised "More stars than there are in the heavens." The star system vanished and after that, Metro very nearly vanished, too. It's a ghost studio today to those of us who remember it in its greatest days.

I was going hat in hand to the old studio, which was changing, to talk to the new boss, whom I didn't know very well. I had no fast lines for this trip, no snappy cracks about Butch Jenkins. I needed help and I was asking for it, humbly.

"Mr. Schary," I said, "I made a mistake leaving Metro."

"Looks that way," Schary said.

I swallowed pride and a lump. "I'm big enough to admit my mistake, and I was hoping you'd be big enough to take me back."

Schary adopted the tone one uses in talking to unemployables, "We'll see if we can find something for you," he said.

I left feeling like two cents, which was just about what my career was worth. In the years with Steifel, my hot career had turned cold. That cost a fortune. I'd been divorced by Betty Jane. More money. The scramble was on. It was almost time to panic. What I needed to come back strong was one good picture. What I got was stuff like My Brother, The Outlaw and Sound Off. I say again, if it needs saying, what I needed was one good picture. It never came.

. . .

I played Korea because I wanted to, or maybe because I wanted to be wanted. I came back and sat, waiting. I married again and again. I bought Elaine the $125,000 home. I was having no trouble spending money. The trouble was obtaining it.

One day a retired harmonica player who walked with a cane came to see me. His name was Maurice Duke and he wanted to manage me. "I'll get you started again," he said.

Sometimes I think that I'm a professional loss. In any business deal where one man makes money and one man loses, I'm the one to lose. It's a touch I seem to have. Sadim—Midas spelled backwards.

I made some cheap, forgettable, forgotten movies for Columbia and then Duke took me to Republic studios, under an arrangement where I was to share in the profits. I made *Twinkle in God's Eye*, a nice little picture, and something called *Jaquar*, with Sabu. I waited for profits but there weren't any. The only thing to share were losses.

We thought of television and I came up with an idea for a series on the life of Daniel Boone. I put $30,000 into a pilot film. Then I found out that no one knew who Daniel Boone was. They all thought he was Davey Crockett. I plowed another $30,000 into a pilot called *Dateline Tokyo*, based on the files of the Tokyo police. The pilot starred Dane Clark. It said good-bye during the introduction.

Two old friends, Blake Edwards and Dick Quine, had come up with the idea for a series for me which they wanted to call *For the Love of Mike*. What I needed was one good picture, but one good television series wouldn't have hurt. "Fine," I told Blake and Dick. "Love to do it."

For the Love of Mike, a fair enough title, turned out to be unavailable. It had been registered by an announcer named Mike Wallace who never, to my knowledge, has used it. We changed our title to *Hey, Mulligan*, and the series went on the air. I was cast as a page boy for a broadcasting company. Joey Foreman was cast as the other page. We hired Joey, a first-class comic, after a brief interview. Joey finished the interview, we told him "maybe" and he left. A few seconds later he came back into the office, saying nothing, but walking on his knees.

Hey, Mulligan wasn't the worst show on TV, nor was it the best. I was a little over age to play a page. I had some ideas about pacing which were wrong. But it wasn't a terrible show. Trouble was the opposition was spectacular. The opposition was Jackie Gleason.

After two weeks of reading the ratings, we knew we were lost. *I* think *Hey, Mulligan* actually ran for thirty-three weeks, but after the first two, lots of people gave up on it. A sponsor gave up on it soon afterwards at a party.

Some television sponsors take liberties with their stars. They expect stars not only to perform, but to do commercials, whistle "Dixie," join them for golf, talk to their salesmen and dance with their wives. Some sponsors do, not all. Bill Dietrich, president of Jolly Green Giant company, one of our sponsors, was a pleasant man. When difficulty came it was with our other sponsor, the makers of Pillsbury Flour.

The Pillsbury family mansion, which makes most other mansions look like garages, is somewhere in the Midwest. I forget—I guess the psychological term is block—exactly where. Maurice Duke and I were commanded to the Pillsbury estate one weekend, and when we got there we saw more servants than we'd ever seen in one place before. We didn't realize that there were two more servants than we'd counted. The extra two were Maurice Duke and Mickey Rooney.

Even though the show had been going badly, Mrs. Pillsbury seemed very glad to meet us. "We've got a chance to keep the show going," Duke whispered. "Just be nice to everybody."

There was dancing, lots of booze and a whole bagful of Pillsburys. I smiled and was as pleasant as I could be. Then late in the evening one Pillsbury asked me to play the piano and sing.

"No," I said, "but thanks for asking. I just don't feel up to it right now."

Another Pillsbury glared at me. "What do you mean you won't?" he said. "We own you."

No longer pleasant, I said, "You don't own anybody, pal."

The Pillsburys arose in wrath. That threw the final shovel of earth on *Hey, Mulligan*, my first television series.

I was spending money fast, too fast. Since my career had turned around, turned away from the blithe days of my youth, I had married and been divorced by Martha Vickers. That was expensive. I had married Elaine Mahnken. That was expensive. And all the while I was fighting, telling myself that no, I wasn't through as a star, hell I was only in my thirties, that maybe I had a lot of breaks when I was a child, but I still had to have one more coming.

I didn't live as though there were no tomorrows. I lived as though it were yesterday. A matter of pride. Just because Hollywood seemed to be against me, because I couldn't work at my trade, was I going to pull back and live like a frugal hermit? Hell, no. I was going to live like Mickey Rooney, movie star. Never mind where the money was coming from. Never mind where the money was going. I was a movie star. I could spend what I wanted. The hell with balance sheets and ledgers.

Duke and I parted. I did a good play for CBS called *The Comedian,* and with a new manager, Red Doff, I began to get more work. But my career didn't resume in a day. And meanwhile the money was going and my marriage to Elaine was on the rocks and I began to run up bills everywhere. I didn't duck any, which isn't saying that I paid them all. I paid what I could, which wasn't much. First I had a platoon of creditors. Then a battalion. Then a regiment. Then a whole damn Army. And at the head of the Army, wrapped in red, white and blue, stood the Government of the United States.

It's easy to fall behind in tax payments. The Government isn't like a grocer. If you're two weeks late with a check, the Government doesn't call you. You fall behind, further and further behind, and one day the Government gets around to noticing that it has some money due from

M. Rooney, actor. I fell roughly $100,000 behind and then the man from Internal Revenue came around, reasonable, to be sure, but forceful.

He had a message for me from my government that went like this:

Mr. Rooney, we understand you are having some financial difficulties. We know you owe us a great deal. Now we don't want to persecute you. That's not our way. All we want is the money you owe us. We won't destroy you. Instead we'll be your partner. That way will be easiest for everyone.

The Government proposed conditions. I was not to have a checking account. I didn't seem to be responsible with checks. I was not to have a savings account. I didn't seem to understand what savings meant. When I earned money, the pay was to go directly to my lawyer, Dermot Long. He was to call a man at the Internal Revenue office. Dermot and the tax man would then decide what should be done with my money. A percentage would go for back taxes. A percentage would go toward current taxes. The remainder would be placed in an account which Dermot supervised. Checks would be valid only if they were signed by Dermot and by the father of Barbara Thomason, Mrs. Mickey Rooney number five. Checks signed by Mickey Rooney were worthless.

The Government isn't like a grocer. They don't call when you're two weeks late. But when the Government does get around to calling, it makes up for lost time in a hurry. The government man is armed. He's the law.

My partnership with the United States Government has

helped buy rocket fuel, keep the White House painted white, cover the expense accounts of Congressmen, and gas-up helicopters in Vietnam. It has, also, taken so much of my income that I haven't been able to pay much for Mickey Rooney.

Big Uncle was happy. He was getting his. But the other creditors were closing in rapidly. I hated the idea of bankruptcy. It smacked of irresponsibility and failure. But the creditors were moving and I had to keep Big Uncle happy and there just wasn't enough money to go around.

Dermot made up a list for me to study one day. It was the list that totaled $346,513.12. Knowing you owe money is one thing. Seeing your debts on paper, seeing the names of all your creditors assembled, like the names of characters from some disjointed nightmare, is quite another. Dermot showed me the list and I studied it.

There was some back alimony. I knew that. But it was a shock to discover that I owed Mrs. Rooney No. 4 $19,500.

One of my managers had talked me into an investment. Pay television, he'd said, was the coming thing. I didn't have much money, but he could raise some from a bank. I knew pay TV hadn't come yet. I knew that I owed something. It was a shock to discover that for a bad investment I owed the Citizens National Bank and Trust Company a good round $25,000.

I was getting bills from a lawyer named Max Gilford. He was lawyer to Mrs. Rooney No. 4. I hadn't been paying attention to what he sent me. It was a shock to learn that I owed Max Gilford a flat $15,000.

I owed the William Morris Agency $11,357.17. I owed another agency, Goldstone Tobias, $10,000. I owed a publicity firm $6,700. But not all the bills were big.

I owed a grocer $384.53. I owed Martha, Mrs. Rooney No. 3, $450 in child support payments. I owed a trade paper, in which I'd taken an advertisement, $250. But not all the other bills were small. Some were medium sized.

I owed a furrier $1,889 on a $4,300 leopard coat I'd bought for my wife Barbara. I'd bought it, but I couldn't maintain the payments. I owed a car rental company $971.43. I needed a car but, it developed, couldn't afford one. I owed a man named Frank Sennes $5,917.67, which was disputed. I'd agreed to play his club, the Moulin Rouge, under certain conditions, such as good lighting for my act. Sennes didn't meet the conditions. I canceled the act and he hit me with a bill. As I say, that's one bill I challenged. Still it was there. Finally I adjusted this one to our mutual satisfaction.

I owed a doctor $750, and a whole passel of lawyers something over $30,000. I owed. I owed. I owed.

But mostly, and worst of all, was what I owed to a production company. It was a company whose principal asset had been my own talent. It was called Fryman Productions. When I needed money, I tapped my own company. I needed money often. I tapped deep.

There, on Dermot's list, was the daddy of all my debts. I owed Fryman Productions $168,000.

. . .

"The only thing," Dermot was saying, in his office on Hollywood Boulevard, "is to go to the cleaners."

"I don't want bankruptcy," I said.

"I can't keep holding them off, Mick. You owe too much to too many people."

"If I go bankrupt, the scandal will wreck me."

"It won't, Mick," Dermot said. "Going bankrupt is no disgrace. And, besides, you haven't any choice."

I filed for bankruptcy. The next day the story was all over the newspapers. The next day all the papers were thrown out. As I should have known, the story of my bankruptcy, as the newspapers saw it, was only a one-day wonder.

How can one man go through $12 million is what you want to know. It's what I want to know myself. No one in the world can tell you what he's done with every penny in his lifetime. My case is different. I can't tell you what I've done with every $100,000. And maybe that's how. Maybe that's the way to go through $12 million.

Everything moved in funny ways. I was a child actor, making money before I went to school. But I was never the top child actor. I was never as big as Shirley Temple. Then I was in my teens. That's supposed to finish a child actor. Temple, Jackie Coogan and the rest went downhill after puberty. But not me. When I was supposed to be slipping, I became bigger than I'd ever been and the money came faster than any ten children could spend it.

Finally, I was a man. The Government said so. I could vote. The State of California said so. I could marry. But in manhood, in my immature manhood, I made my childish mistakes. It was almost as if, never a child, I turned childish as a man. The Steifel deal. And there I was in my prime, a bad drug on the uncertain actor's market. What the hell was this? I was Mickey Rooney. I was a star. I could damn well do what I pleased, damn well go where I pleased, damn well spend what I pleased. So I spent and I lent and all of a sudden, when those old trusts' annual payment came due, there was a man from the Bureau of Internal Revenue. "I'm sorry, Mr. Rooney. The Government has a prior claim on your trust funds." I spent and I lent and I married and damn it, I don't know how, I went through $12 million. You see, if I knew how I did it, I'd know a lot about money. If I knew how I did it, I wouldn't have done it in the first place. Ask a drunk where all the booze has gone. That's like asking me about my money. You can probably figure out the answer. It's the same for the two of us.

7 [*] *Not in Demand*

Night
Hear the night
Hear the night tick.
Hear how still it sounds.
Fill your being through with all you tried
    to do and didn't.
No wonder you've no time . . .
It couldn't wait, the night.

M.R.

I

So we come to it. We come to it at last, man's ancient and
most beloved enemy, eternal and most despised friend.
We have transcended the counterplots of love and lust
and money. We have come at last to life.

My life—a poor thing, but mine own. My life—
wretched, triumphant, luminous, pallid, angry, timorous,
mine own. Always mine own.

I think I understand my life. A man can live a hundred

years, wandering everywhere, and never approach understanding. Put a man in a prison fashioned by himself and
by others, put a man in a prison, lock him there with his
talent, hidden from all the world, and that man must
approach understanding. Or die.

I sat in that prison for ten years of my manhood. Sometimes I drank. Sometimes I strayed. Sometimes I hid from
truth with pills. It was a big prison, high and wide. But in
that prison, there were days and weeks and months when
I was sentenced to think. Thus understanding comes, after
great battles.

If this were a movie, and not a book, I'd have some
childhood music tinkling here. There'd be a little boy's
song, tinkling from a wind-up phonograph, the kind they
had when I, and maybe you, were young. And while this
music played, there'd be this man, puffy around the eyes,
a little jowly, and just starting to grow bald. And the
music of childhood would play and the man would lift a
bottle to his mouth. A grown-up bottle, big and amber.
He'd lift the bottle to his mouth and miss and hit his
cheek and try again, while whiskey trickled down his
face. He'd find his mouth and slug the whiskey down and
fall across the bed, face up. His eyes would roll once,
dully, before the man passed out. And all the while, as the
man twitched into unconsciousness, the little boy's song
would tinkle in our ears.

The murder of innocence. Innocence died this afternoon, at 3:15, Pacific Standard Time. Innocence died, the
victim of life.

Then, as the man snorted in his stupor, we'd have a flashback. Not all the way to boyhood. The music sings of boyhood. We'd flash back to some things of which the man is proud. We'd want the audience to know that this unconscious man has not passed his years snorting unpleasantly, lying awkwardly upon an unmade bed.

This is not a movie, so there can be no music. Movie or book, I am, or was, that man.

II

On the bed, amid unconsciousness, moments of consciousness interrupted, and there were days when I wandered forth, days that tell hard because of pride. No one wants to remember too much of himself or even of others. Perhaps that's why so many of us run away.

Temporarily, I had abandoned bottle and bed and I was working again. The year? 1956. I wasn't doing the work that I wanted. I was playing night clubs. Oh, I can play clubs and, Lord knows, maybe some day I'll have to play them again. But what I am in my own eye is an actor. I don't think of myself as someone who struts before an audience that is picking at its beef and shouting above the ice rattling in half-empty highball glasses. I'd rather act.

But in 1956 this club work came and I was told be glad you've got it, and I wasn't, but I said I was and set off for the Calneva Lodge in Lake Tahoe and worked for a while and then it was time to drive down to Las Vegas for a second date.

At Vegas, I was supposed to play the New Frontier Hotel. Four weeks. Seventy thousand dollars. That sounds like a lot and would be, except you know that even $100,000 isn't much after its been sliced and strained. You know. I didn't.

Judy Garland was closing at the New Frontier the night before I opened. A Judy who had grown older and more troubled. Myself as she. I don't remember if we spoke. I don't remember if either of us dared. Judy and I and Andy Hardy now nearer the state of dust, which is what happens to old celluloid and people.

It must have bothered me, seeing Judy at work in her bad time, seeing that reflection of part of myself. I had to get out of there. I had to get away from the reflection. I had to take a drink and run, and where could I run to? Welcome to Las Vegas, friends. Run right over here or run right over there. It doesn't matter where you try to run. You end up at the tables.

Here, or there, was an actor I knew, John Carroll. You may have seen him. Mustache. Often a heavy.

"Hi, John."

"Hi, Mick."

"Say, John. Who's got the action?"

Carroll walked me over to a big, loud, laughing Texan, and ol' Tex laughed loud and said that Waal, it was sho' nice to meet Mickey Rooney and it sho' would be nicer if Mick would join him fo' a li'l fun.

Fun was the name of the game. Fun and forgetfulness. Helluva game. Bigger than Scrabble.

"How much?" I said.

"Hundred apiece," the Texan said. He was a banker and now he was talking business.

"I'm you're podner," I said, talking Texan. Dice chattered. Soon my hundreds were gone.

What the hell, I thought. It didn't matter. Have another drink, ol' Tex. See that booth over there? I just sign a little chit and they bring me all the chips I need. Right now they owe me seventy thousand dollars.

"Five hundred apiece," the Texan said, "and I'll buy the drinks." He wasn't trying to take me. He was just a very rich man out on bat who wanted to have a collaborator. Could have been me. Might have been the devil.

The Texan snapped to attention. "Let's put in some real money and get our losses back. What do you say, Mick?"

I felt high-spirited. I'd been drinking Scotch. As a matter of fact, I *was* high-spirited. "That's the way I like to hear a man talk."

"Ten thousand," the Texan said. "Five for me. Five for you."

"Podner, we're gonna ride high."

Don't fight cold dice. I know it. You know it. A man knows the real feel of cold dice in his hand the way he knows, in his heart, how he's doing with the girl who matters. He knows, but he may not admit. A crowd was gathering. Tex and I, we had the action. Except the dice were cold.

That ten thousand went and we looked at each other, not long enough, not hard enough. "Should we take another ten?" Tex said.

"Might as well," I said, touched by doubt.

Behind me a voice said, "Don't be crazy, Mick. Why don't you quit for the night?"

"Quit for the night! Do you think I'm a quitter? Before this night's up, I'll make a hundred thousand dollars."

Not that night, or any night, I'm afraid, but challenge a gambler when his luck is down and he'll gamble twice as hard.

That next ten thousand went and more and more and more and all the while the crowd gathered. Was I playing to an audience? Was I tearing myself apart? Or both? Or neither? I don't know. But before that night was over, I lost $50,000 at the New Frontier, pulled out for El Rancho Vegas and lost $5,000 more. Fifty-five thousand in a single reckless night. Morning rose above Las Vegas, staining the desert sky, restoring sanity. By the time that morning came, it was too late.

III

That was Vegas, which isn't my town. Maybe it isn't anybody's town. Maybe it belongs to the machines and to the tables and the flat green fields of rattling craps. What about my own town? What about Hollywood, California?

You're never really big in Hollywood. You're only as big as your last picture or series. And above all, the cardinal sin is being broke. The hands that will help you are few while the hands that help themselves are many. This may be true in all industry, but in the business world it doesn't hide behind the façade of friendship.

One of the greatest hurts was when I received an invitation to an Academy Awards dinner, and maybe that isn't the most important thing in the world, but it means something in Hollywood, and it was a place to go. I was glad to have a place to go. I received a phone call from Johnny Green, the conductor, who informed me that he had been elected as the man to tell me not to go to the dinner. It appeared that my presence might be detrimental to the industry and my invitation had been rescinded.

How low had the mighty mite fallen?

I never knock my town. It's no different from any place else. It's a helluva place to be when you're a winner.

IV

What about television? Where was television when the movie business decided I was finished? I'll tell you a little about TV.

A great entertainer can make an audience laugh or cry. A no-talent entertainer stands in front of an audience and laughs or cries himself. You've watched TV. You understand. Bad joke. Canned laughter. Heh, heh, goes the entertainer. *And then there was the time heh, heh . . .*

I'm waiting for the night when all the cans of laughter run dry.

This is the great era of no-talent talent. Never before have so many people watching performers settled for so little performance. Why? The big thing may be television, which is free. Anything that's free doesn't seem to be worth very much. A man who goes to the theater can have ten, twenty or fifty dollars invested in having himself and his friends entertained. A man going to the movies may invest ten dollars. He has left his house and gone out with a certain commitment and he wants to be moved or amused whether it's something grand like *Hamlet* or something small like *Andy Hardy*. When you're paying to be entertained, dammit, they'd better entertain you.

Television is different. The man sits in the living room with a can of beer in one hand and a newspaper on his lap and a wife complaining about the family budget and every few minutes a child breaks in to ask some questions about algebra which the man didn't understand twenty-five years before and hasn't been studying very hard since. Now suppose into this happy domestic scene a great talent thunders on to the 21-inch screen. Suppose Paul Muni thunders on, raging against oppression or for right, filling the screen and even the room with his greatness. What happens?

The man drops the beer, the newspaper slides to the floor, his wife subsides and he throws the algebra book into the playroom. The family routine has been disrupted. Paul Muni has broken into the home and altered the pattern of home life.

Do people want this? Not all of them, to be sure. But some of them? According to the TV powers that be, almost nobody does. Instead of creating in television a thundering new force, the people who own the TV shops have created something tepid, inoffensive, unchallenging.

Consider the same scene as matters stand: same man, same wife, same beer can, same paper, same child, even the same bloody algebra questions. There is no Paul Muni

on the screen. Instead we see a nameless, faceless, vapid
girl whose best previous acting performance was per-
suading some idiot, or entrepreneur, that she deserved the
part. The leading man, opposite the faceless girl, looks
familiar and is, because he has the same looks as a dozen
other television actors. In fact, he was chosen because he
resembled someone someone else liked last year. The
script has been hacked out by a writer in a hurry. A
cluster of people has hovered during rehearsal to make
certain that anything strong appearing in the story is
diluted or killed. So that man in the living room gets
vapid, faceless, diluted television. His home life is undisturbed; he says to his wife, "All right, all right. You can
have an extra ten to run the house." He sips at his beer
and notes in the newspaper that Dick Tracy has battled
his way out of another tough one. The man says to the
child, "If I solve that algebra problem, you won't be learning yourself, will you, son? Solve it on your own. That's
what school is for." The man is undisturbed, but if that's
what acting is about, leaving people undisturbed, I'm
going to open that window cleaning business for real.

The public responds to what it sees. Television has
conditioned a lot of the public to expect tepid entertainment. The public as a mass has grown less demanding of
and less interested in individual talent. I remember great
entertainers: Muni, who played on your emotions the way
Heifetz plays a fiddle; Chaplin (we're not talking politics
here) with his profound sense of the absurd, making you
laugh and wonder all at once; Clark Gable and Gary

Cooper, who flooded the vast screen with presence; Spencer Tracy, always, and still, the great professional. Were they great, these men, only because memory magnifies? I think not.

Consider our existing TV talent. Paar? Beneath consideration. Godfrey? He could sing a little bit and he could talk a great deal. He couldn't act. But people loved him. They'd look up from their living rooms and they'd say, "Look at that. There's old Arthur. He's one of us. Three cheers for Arthur."

I'm not saying there's no talent at all. That wouldn't make sense. Not with people like Buddy Hackett and Sammy Davis, Jr., around. I'm just saying that great talent isn't what TV wants. Be mediocre, that's the name of the game. The hell with calories. Talent don't count.

It's funny. It was TV that saved my career. Not a woman, or a drink, or a pill, or an old buddy. TV, which caters to the mediocre, picked me up and dusted me off. Does that make me mediocre? Often, buddy, and I'm the first one to know it. Often I'm mediocre, or worse. But on the night that TV saved me, I was right.

There was this script they had, up at CBS, by Rod Serling, one of the very best TV writers. It was about an unpleasant performer and I don't know how many actors they tried to get, but as I say, the central figure was unpleasant. So they asked a lot of people, who wanted to seem pleasant, and then at last they had to come to me.

The script is about a comic, loud, kind of dirty, kind of evil. His favorite routine is abusing his brother. Well, this comic's brother has a pretty wife who believes, among other things, in dignity. She wants her husband to stop working with this brother. Stop taking abuse. Become a man.

Of course the comic finds out, and he comes up with a proposition for the lady. He'll ease up on his brother if he can ease into her. He makes his move, keeps needling the brother, and then it's time to worry about new insults to throw at his brother in the next show.

The name of the script was *The Comedian,* and as I played him (and Serling wrote him) he was a monster.

That turned it. I played a monster and all over the country critics seemed to make a discovery. Mickey Rooney knew how to act. Hell, I was grateful. The way the acting business is, all I'd needed was one good performance in one good script. Once that was in, everybody decided that Mickey Rooney knew how to act. TV parts came and work in movies. After a while important movies. *Breakfast at Tiffany's, Requiem for a Heavyweight, It's a Mad, Mad, Mad, Mad World.* With movies and with TV parts, I was working again. I was back in the acting business.

Welcome, Mr. Rooney, they said around 1960. Welcome to the business of acting.

I'm grateful for the welcome, grateful to you all, but here's a surprise, gentlemen. I've been in the business all my life.

They wondered after *The Comedian.* They wonder who the real comedian was. Who was I playing? They guessed it was Jackie Gleason, Phil Silvers, Milton Berle, a little of each. Myself, I don't know. An actor, like a writer, can't say exactly what his creation is. (Although he feels it, which is a different thing.) But this is what I think. I don't think that monster was Gleason, Silvers or Berle. I think that part of him—the bitterness—was me, *i.e.*, Mickey Rooney, *i.e.*, lying around for ten years, *i.e.*, crying for work.

V

It's ridiculous the way things turn around. On the bed, with the booze, semiconscious, I wanted more than anything else to tummul. What's that? A kind of roughhouse entertaining. I've tummuled in a couple of wars.

Most of the time it was easy give-and-take, cracking wise at soldiers who were cracking wise at you, with everybody laughing. It was good because much of the laughter came from what I could do. But there was one day, I remembered on the bed amid the booze, one day I remembered with pride.

Somewhere in France. A day in World War II. A hospital filled with terribly wounded men. An accordionist playing sentimental songs.

"Mickey," a boy was calling. "Mr. Rooney."

I walked over to the boy's bed. He was crying a little. "What's the matter, buddy?" I said.

"Would you ask the accordionist to stop playing? It's getting me upset. Tomorrow they're going to cut off my leg."

What to say, what to say, what to say?

I stopped the music. "So," I told the soldier, "you're going to be a famous leading man, huh?"

He stopped crying. "What do you mean?"

"You know Herbert Marshall?"

"Yeah. That great English guy."

"A very smooth gentleman, pal. Suave. He ends up with all the leading ladies a guy like me can't touch."

"He does?"

"Well, the truth is he lost a leg in the First World War and did that stop him? Hell no. He's got glamour."

The soldier grinned, and the next day they cut off his leg, as they had to, but my tummuling helped get him through the night.

That was what I remembered through my wasted years. Let them all say I couldn't act. On the one day of my life when acting was most important, I'd come through. I gave my best performance to an audience of one crying boy.

I helped get him through the night and because life works in funny circles, he got me through many nights himself. He did, or his memory.

But that was ending now. I'd played *The Comedian*. Other people were learning Mickey Rooney could act. It was time to get up from the bed. Break the bottle. Kick the pills. Get out there. An audience is waiting.

I was ready.

Night was over.

It was day.

8 * *The Pause*

In writing my story, I had to pause. A pause of over one year. Thank God it was the pause that refreshed. Refreshed what? My life.

Largely because of that period, my career has rebounded. It is still climbing. Further—and amazing—I face no more lawsuits. I owe no man a cent.

As I write, I sit in a comfortable home in Beverly Hills, a home which is larger than some of the others that did not bring happiness. This home is completely and beautifully furnished. But best of all are Barbara and my lovely children, Kelly, Kerry, Kim and Kyle. Around me flows a warmth that has driven out the chill of bitterness.

There is milady Barbara, who has become the fifth, and only, Mrs. Rooney. Barbara, blond, lovely (and not tall). It did not come easily, our love, but when it came, it was as if there had been no other. No Ava. No Betty Jane. No Martha. No Elaine. Only Barbara.

Four children run. My children. It is an old story, the

one of father and children, not one that I could presume to tell again.

And into my home comes my son Timmy, who worked with me on a TV series not long ago. Timmy's brother Mickey, Jr., is recording and successful. B.J. can well be proud of them. Certainly I am.

Teddy, my son by Martha, stops over to see his dad from time to time. Someday he too will be on his way. The wheel of fortune seems to have reversed. God's in his heaven; all's right with the world. Here, as I sit with my wife and children, it is as if I had found the land of lost contentment.

Forty-four years it has taken me to get here. A long journey, but a worthwhile one, I think.

Financially, I'm safe. Even after filing the bankruptcy, I still owed $150,000. But by constant hard work and successful engagements I've paid my debts. The one big debt, to Internal Revenue, was the bugaboo. I had managed to reduce this to $97,000, but under our present tax structure I could not possibly earn enough to pay current taxes and liquidate this liability in a single lifetime. And I certainly did not wish to be accountable to the Internal Revenue Service forever. As individuals, the I.R.S. boys were wonderful to me, but I never felt free. There had to be an out. There was. My trust fund.

This trust fund, established in my teens, was a so-called spendthrift trust. I could draw the interest annually, but it could not be rescinded, invaded, or the principal paid to me until I was sixty years old. It was set up for my old age. As things developed, it may help *your* old age. I used it to pay my back taxes.

The financial intricacies elude me. All I know is that my attorney prepared a petition for release of sufficient funds to pay those taxes. He pointed out to the court that the $97,000 I owed "would equal the accumulated interest due on said sum if it were allowed to go on the seventeen-year period pending release of said funds." So that when I received the trust, I'd pay up my back interest and still owe the $97,000. Thank the Lord for that judge. It made sense. He released the funds, and I paid my taxes.

I've paid my alimony, child support, creditors and church. I hope to repay you through good acting in the years to come.

I'm determined never to get into that position again, and I'm certain that my business manager, Sam Singer, and my attorney, Derm Long, won't allow me to. I want to acquire substantial assets for the protection of Barbara and the children. My lesson is learned. Cost: $12 million. Again worthwhile.

How do I live? Quite dully, really. When I work, I embrace the make-believe of acting, riding off early toward a set to spend hours producing a few feet of film.

On days when I don't work, I usually hover around the house, doing the small significant things that comprise a husband and father. Or perhaps scribble a synopsis for a picture. As I write this, I have three commitments. Two of them are my stories. You can find me out rooting for the Dodgers and visiting Santa Anita occasionally. However, I am constantly on the move. TV shows in New York, a picture in Beirut, Lebanon. Personal appearances in Washington, D.C., Houston, Lake Tahoe, Hot Springs, Puerto Rico—and now probably soon, Australia. A picture coming up in Ireland. Another one in England. If Bob Hope has his Valpack—Rooney has his kit bag. It's hard on Barbara but she has the good sense to realize that the road to security for her is the highroad of travel for me. So I move around. After a tempestuous journey, contentment.

The excitement is now in my mind. It is in thoughts that rush and spill of things I yet shall do. I grow older, perhaps seemingly more tame, certainly more content, but the drives that have hurtled me remain. I think a lot more now. I think and plan.

The bitterness that is in this book is only because I know the me that might have been. I also know the me that still can be.

The key that unlocks the world, will I ever find it? Does such a key exist? Perhaps it's love.

As for my life, Andy Hardy said, "Gee."

Puck said:

> *If we shadows have offended*
> *Think but this and all is mended.*

Puck had a better writer going for him, but I played them both. I wish I knew more about acting, living, writing. But Hemingway knew, and did it help him?

—Have I forgotten to insult any phony? Beg pardon.

—Have I forgotten to praise any stand-up guy? Beg pardon.

—One thing for which I never will beg pardon: My life.

—Oh, I have been cruel, insensitive, immature. My sins are as long as your arm and longer than mine.

—I have lived, lusted and laughed and wasted my time.

—I have gambled, too much, and tomorrow may do it again.

—I shall try not to, but no promises. My life has been one long gamble out on the stage. It's hard to gamble there, but I've not been afraid. Working out there on a stage, I like the odds.

What are we doing, with all this warmth around us, conducting a wake? Is Mickey Rooney dead? The hell he is. The boy grows older but not a whit more dead.

Look, I've made my mistakes yesterday and today, and tomorrow, as surely as I sit here, I'll make mistakes again. But I haven't pulled back, or bowed to fear. I live hard, from the toenails up. I will make my mistakes, but fewer, I think, as I wrestle this thing called life day after day.

Mistakes won't frighten me for as long as I have the courage to try. Lord, may I keep the courage to be wrong for all the rest of my days.

I like this thing called life.

I'm not afraid.

Even Einstein died with something more to learn.